Borneo, Celebes, Aru

Celebes, 1856

ALFRED RUSSEL WALLACE

Borneo, Celebes, Aru

GREAT
JOURNEYS

TED SMART

PENGUIN BOOKS

Published by the Penguin Group
Penguin Books Ltd, 80 Strand, London WC2R 0RL, England
Penguin Group (USA) Inc., 375 Hudson Street, New York, New York 10014, USA
Penguin Group (Canada), 90 Eglinton Avenue East, Suite 700, Toronto, Ontario, Canada M4P 2Y3
(a division of Pearson Penguin Canada Inc.)
Penguin Ireland, 25 St Stephen's Green, Dublin 2, Ireland (a division of Penguin Books Ltd)
Penguin Group (Australia), 250 Camberwell Road, Camberwell, Victoria 3124, Australia
(a division of Pearson Australia Group Pty Ltd)
Penguin Books India Pvt Ltd, 11 Community Centre, Panchsheel Park, New Delhi – 110 017, India
Penguin Group (NZ), 67 Apollo Drive, Rosedale, North Shore 0632, New Zealand
(a division of Pearson New Zealand Ltd)
Penguin Books (South Africa) (Pty) Ltd, 24 Sturdee Avenue, Rosebank, Johannesburg 2196, South Africa

Penguin Books Ltd, Registered Offices: 80 Strand, London WC2R 0RL, England

www.penguin.com

The Malay Archipelago first published 1869
This extract published in Penguin Books 2007

3

All rights reserved

Inside-cover maps by Jeff Edwards

Typeset by Rowland Phototypesetting Ltd, Bury St Edmunds, Suffolk
Printed in England by Clays Ltd, St Ives plc

ISBN: 978-0-141-02548-3

This edition produced for The Book People Ltd,
Hall Wood Avenue, Haydock, St. Helens, WA11 9UL

Contents

The Malay Archipelago by Alfred Russel Wallace (1823–1913) is one of the great works of nineteenth-century literature: a discursive, mesmerizing, beautifully descriptive, occasionally offensive work of art by a great biologist and writer. Having worked with Walter Henry Bates in the Amazon (and lost all his collections in a catastrophic fire at sea), Wallace spent 1854 to 1862 wandering across the East Indies (now Malaysia and Indonesia) from Sumatra in the west to New Guinea in the east, earning his living as a bird-skin collector. It was while he was in the Aru Islands, off the coast of New Guinea, that (quite independently of Darwin) Wallace realized the true 'origin of species'.

It has proved nightmarishly hard to extract sections from *The Malay Archipelago* as each island on which Wallace lived has its own remarkable atmosphere. This selection begins with his account of the 'Wallace Line', which he was the first to identify (his analysis predates any conception of the role of continental drift). This is followed by his famous and horrifying description of his orang-utan hunting expeditions and then by incidents in the Sarawak interior, Celebes (now Sulawesi) and the Aru Islands.

The Theory of the 'Wallace Line'

[...]

It is now generally admitted that the present distribution of living things on the surface of the earth is mainly the result of the last series of changes that it has undergone. Geology teaches us that the surface of the land, and the distribution of land and water, is everywhere slowly changing. It further teaches us that the forms of life which inhabit that surface have, during every period of which we possess any record, been also slowly changing.

It is not now necessary to say anything about how either of those changes took place; as to that, opinions may differ; but as to the fact that the changes themselves have occurred, from the earliest geological ages down to the present day, and are still going on, there is no difference of opinion. Every successive stratum of sedimentary rock, sand, or gravel, is a proof that changes of level have taken place; and the different species of animals and plants, whose remains are found in these deposits, prove that corresponding changes did occur in the organic world. Taking, therefore, these two series of changes for granted, most of the present peculiarities and anomalies in the distribution of species may be directly traced to them. In our own islands, with a very few trifling exceptions, every quadruped, bird, reptile, insect, and plant, is found also on the adjacent continent. In the small islands of Sardinia and Corsica, there are some quadrupeds and insects, and many plants, quite peculiar. In Ceylon, more closely connected to India than Britain is to Europe, many animals and plants are different from those found in India, and peculiar to the island. In the Galapagos Islands, almost every indigenous living thing is peculiar to them, though closely resembling other kinds found in the nearest parts of the American continent.

Most naturalists now admit that these facts can only be explained by the greater or less lapse of time since the islands were upraised from beneath the ocean, or were separated from the nearest land; and this will be generally (though not always) indicated by the depth of the intervening sea. The enormous thickness of many marine deposits through wide areas shows that subsidence has often continued (with intermitting periods of repose) during epochs of immense duration. The depth of sea produced by such subsidence will therefore generally be a measure of time; and in like manner, the change which organic forms have undergone is a measure of time. When we make proper allowance for the continued introduction of new animals and plants from surrounding countries by those natural means of dispersal which have been so well explained by Sir Charles Lyell and Mr Darwin, it is remarkable how closely these two measures correspond. Britain is separated from the continent by a very shallow sea, and only in a very few cases have our animals or plants begun to show a difference from the corresponding continental species. Corsica and

Sardinia, divided from Italy by a much deeper sea, present a much greater difference in their organic forms. Cuba, separated from Yucatan by a wider and deeper strait, differs more markedly, so that most of its productions are of distinct and peculiar species; while Madagascar, divided from Africa by a deep channel three hundred miles wide, possesses so many peculiar features as to indicate separation at a very remote antiquity, or even to render it doubtful whether the two countries have ever been absolutely united.

Returning now to the Malay Archipelago, we find that all the wide expanse of sea which divides Java, Sumatra, and Borneo from each other, and from Malacca and Siam, is so shallow that ships can anchor in any part of it, since it rarely exceeds forty fathoms in depth; and if we go as far as the line of a hundred fathoms, we shall include the Philippine Islands and Bali, east of Java. If, therefore, these islands have been separated from each other and the continent by subsidence of the intervening tracts of land, we should conclude that the separation has been comparatively recent, since the depth to which the land has subsided is so small. It is also to be remarked that the great chain of active volcanoes in Sumatra and Java furnishes us with a sufficient cause for such subsidence, since the enormous masses of matter they have thrown out would take away the foundations of the surrounding district; and this may be the true explanation of the often-noticed fact that volcanoes and volcanic chains are always near the sea. The subsidence they produce around them will, in time, make a sea, if one does not already exist.

But, it is when we examine the zoology of these countries that we find what we most require – evidence of a very striking character that these great islands must have once formed a part of the continent, and could only have been separated at a very recent geological epoch. The elephant and tapir of Sumatra and Borneo, the rhinoceros of Sumatra and the allied species of Java, the wild cattle of Borneo and the kind long supposed to be peculiar to Java, are now all known to inhabit some part or other of Southern Asia. None of these large animals could possibly have passed over the arms of the sea which now separate these countries, and their presence plainly indicates that a land communication must have existed since the origin of the species. Among the smaller mammals, a considerable portion are common to each island and the continent; but the vast physical changes that must have occurred during the breaking up and subsidence of such extensive regions have led to the extinction of some in one or more of the islands, and in some cases there seems also to have been time for a change of species to have taken place. Birds and insects illustrate the same view, for every family and almost every genus of these groups found in any of the islands occurs also on the Asiatic continent, and in a great number of cases the species are exactly identical. Birds offer us one of the best means of determining the law of distribution; for though at first sight it would appear that the watery boundaries which keep out the land quadrupeds could be easily passed over by birds, yet practically it is not so; for if we leave out the aquatic tribes which are preeminently wanderers, it is found that the others (and especially the Passeres, or true perching-birds, which form the vast majority) are generally as strictly limited by straits and arms of the sea as are quadrupeds themselves. As an instance, among the islands of which I am now speaking, it is a remarkable fact that Java possesses numerous birds which never pass over to Sumatra, though they are separated by a strait only fifteen miles wide, and with islands in mid-channel. Java, in fact, possesses more birds and insects peculiar to itself than either Sumatra or Borneo, and this would indicate that it was earliest separated from the continent; next in organic individuality is Borneo, while Sumatra is so nearly identical in all its animal forms with the peninsula of Malacca, that we may safely conclude it to have been the most recently dismembered island.

The general result therefore, at which we arrive, is that the great islands of Java, Sumatra, and Borneo resemble in their natural productions the adjacent parts of the continent, almost as much as such widely-separated districts could be expected to do even if they still formed a part of Asia; and this close resemblance, joined with the fact of the wide extent of sea which separates them being so uniformly and remarkably shallow, and lastly, the existence of the extensive range of volcanoes in Sumatra and Java, which have poured out vast quantities of subterranean matter and have built up extensive plateaux and lofty mountain ranges, thus furnishing a vera causa for a parallel line of subsidence – all lead irresistibly to the conclusion that at a very recent geological epoch, the continent of Asia extended far beyond its present limits in a south-easterly direction, including the islands of Java, Sumatra, and Borneo, and probably reaching as far as the present 100-fathom line of soundings.

The Philippine Islands agree in many respects with Asia and the other islands, but present some anomalies, which seem to indicate that they were separated at an earlier period, and have since been subject to many revolutions in their physical geography.

Turning our attention now to the remaining portion of the Archipelago, we shall find that all the islands from Celebes and Lombock eastward exhibit almost as close a resemblance to Australia and New Guinea as the Western Islands do to Asia. It is well known that the natural productions of Australia differ from those of Asia more than those of any of the four ancient quarters of the world differ from each other. Australia, in fact, stands alone: it possesses no apes or monkeys, no cats or tigers, wolves, bears, or hyenas; no deer or antelopes, sheep or oxen; no elephant, horse, squirrel, or rabbit; none, in short, of those familiar types of quadruped which are met with in every other part of the world. Instead of these, it has Marsupials only: kangaroos and opossums; wombats and the duckbilled Platypus. In birds it is almost as peculiar. It has no woodpeckers and no pheasants – families which exist in every other part of the world; but instead of them it has the mound-making brush-turkeys, the honeysuckers, the cockatoos, and the brush-tongued lories, which are found nowhere else upon the globe. All these strik-ing peculiarities are found also in those islands which form the Austro-Malayan division of the Archipelago.

The great contrast between the two divisions of the Archipelago is nowhere so abruptly exhibited as on passing from the island of Bali to that of Lombock, where the two regions are in closest proximity. In Bali we have barbets, fruit-thrushes, and woodpeckers; on passing over to Lombock these are seen no more, but we have abundance of cockatoos, honeysuckers, and brush-turkeys, which are equally unknown in Bali, or any island further west. [I was informed, however, that there were a few cockatoos at one spot on the west of Bali, showing that the intermingling of the productions of these islands is now going on.] The strait is here fifteen miles wide, so that we may pass in two hours from one great division of the earth to another, differing as essentially in their animal life as Europe does from America. If we travel from Java or Borneo to Celebes or the Moluccas, the difference is still more striking. In the first, the forests abound in monkeys of many kinds, wild cats, deer, civets, and otters, and numerous varieties of squirrels are constantly met with. In the latter none of these occur; but the prehensile-tailed Cuscus is almost the only terrestrial mammal seen, except wild pigs, which are found in all the islands, and deer (which have probably been recently introduced) in Celebes and the Moluccas. The birds which are most abundant in the Western Islands are woodpeckers, barbets, trogons, fruit-thrushes, and leaf-thrushes; they are seen daily, and form the great ornithological features of the country. In the Eastern Islands these are absolutely unknown, honeysuckers and small lories being the most common birds, so that the naturalist feels himself in a new world, and can hardly realize that he has passed from the one region to the other in a few days, without ever being out of sight of land.

The inference that we must draw from these facts is, undoubtedly, that the whole of the islands eastwards beyond Java and Borneo do essentially form a part of a former Australian or Pacific continent, although some of them may never have been actually joined to it. This continent must have been broken up not only before the Western Islands were separated from Asia, but probably before the extreme southeastern portion of Asia was raised above the waters of the ocean; for a great part of the land of Borneo and Java is known to be geologically of quite recent formation, while the very great difference of species, and in many cases of genera also, between the productions of the Eastern Malay Islands and Australia, as well as the great depth of the sea now separating them, all point to a comparatively long period of isolation.

It is interesting to observe among the islands themselves how a shallow sea always intimates a recent land connection. The Aru Islands, Mysol, and Waigiou, as well as Jobie, agree with New Guinea in their species of mammalia and birds much more closely than they do with the Moluccas, and we find that they are all united to New Guinea by a shallow sea. In fact, the 100-fathom line round New Guinea marks out accurately the range of the true Paradise birds.

It is further to be noted – and this is a very interesting

point in connection with theories of the dependence of special forms of life on external conditions – that this division of the Archipelago into two regions characterized by a striking diversity in their natural productions does not in any way correspond to the main physical or climatal divisions of the surface. The great volcanic chain runs through both parts, and appears to produce no effect in assimilating their productions. Borneo closely resembles New Guinea not only in its vast size and its freedom from volcanoes, but in its variety of geological structure, its uniformity of climate, and the general aspect of the forest vegetation that clothes its surface. The Moluccas are the counterpart of the Philippines in their volcanic structure, their extreme fertility, their luxuriant forests, and their frequent earthquakes; and Bali with the east end of Java has a climate almost as dry and a soil almost as arid as that of Timor. Yet between these corresponding groups of islands, constructed as it were after the same pattern, subjected to the same climate, and bathed by the same oceans, there exists the greatest possible contrast when we compare their animal productions. Nowhere does the ancient doctrine – that differences or similarities in the various forms of life that inhabit different countries are due to corresponding physical differences or similarities in the countries themselves – meet with so direct and palpable a contradiction. Borneo and New Guinea, as alike physically as two distinct countries can be, are zoologically wide as the poles asunder; while Australia, with its dry winds, its open plains, its stony deserts, and its temperate climate, yet produces birds and quadrupeds which are closely related to those inhabiting the hot damp luxuriant forests, which everywhere clothe the plains and mountains of New Guinea.

[. . .]

One of the chief objects of my travels was to obtain evidence of this nature; and my search after such evidence has been rewarded by great success, so that I have been able to trace out with some probability the past changes which one of the most interesting parts of the earth has undergone. It may be thought that the facts and generalizations here given would have been more appropriately placed at the end rather than at the beginning of a narrative of the travels which supplied the facts. In some cases this might be so, but I have found it impossible to give such an account as I desire of the natural history of the numerous islands and groups of islands in the Archipelago, without constant reference to these generalizations which add so much to their interest. Having given this general sketch of the subject, I shall be able to show how the same principles can be applied to the individual islands of a group, as to the whole Archipelago; and thereby make my account of the many new and curious animals which inhabit them both, more interesting and more instructive than if treated as mere isolated facts.

[. . .]

Borneo: Orangutan Hunting

[...]

One of my chief objects in coming to stay at Simunjon was to see the Orangutan (or great man-like ape of Borneo) in his native haunts, to study his habits, and obtain good specimens of the different varieties and species of both sexes, and of the adult and young animals. In all these objects I succeeded beyond my expectations, and will now give some account of my experience in hunting the Orangutan, or 'Mias,' as it is called by the natives; and as this name is short, and easily pronounced, I shall generally use it in preference to Simia satyrus, or Orangutan.

Just a week after my arrival at the mines, I first saw a Mias. I was out collecting insects, not more than a quarter of a mile from the house, when I heard a rustling in a tree near, and, looking up, saw a large red-haired animal moving slowly along, hanging from the branches by its arms. It passed on from tree to tree until it was lost in the jungle, which was so swampy that I could not follow it. This mode of progression was, however, very unusual, and is more characteristic of the Hylobates than of the Orang. I suppose there was some individual peculiarity in this animal, or the nature of the trees just in this place rendered it the most easy mode of progression.

About a fortnight afterwards I heard that one was

feeding in a tree in the swamp just below the house, and, taking my gun, was fortunate enough to find it in the same place. As soon as I approached, it tried to conceal itself among the foliage; but, I got a shot at it, and the second barrel caused it to fall down almost dead, the two balls having entered the body. This was a male, about half-grown, being scarcely three feet high. On April 26th, I was out shooting with two Dyaks, when we found another about the same size. It fell at the first shot, but did not seem much hurt, and immediately climbed up the nearest tree, when I fired, and it again fell, with a broken arm and a wound in the body. The two Dyaks now ran up to it, and each seized hold of a hand, telling me to cut a pole, and they would secure it. But although one arm was broken and it was only a half-grown animal, it was too strong for these young savages, drawing them up towards its mouth notwithstanding all their efforts, so that they were again obliged to leave go, or they would have been seriously bitten. It now began climbing up the tree again; and, to avoid trouble, I shot it through the heart.

On May 2nd, I again found one on a very high tree, when I had only a small 80-bore gun with me. However, I fired at it, and on seeing me it began howling in a strange voice like a cough, and seemed in a great rage, breaking off branches with its hands and throwing them down, and then soon made off over the tree-tops. I did not care to follow it, as it was swampy, and in parts dangerous, and I might easily have lost myself in the eagerness of pursuit.

On the 12th of May I found another, which behaved in a very similar manner, howling and hooting with rage, and throwing down branches. I shot at it five times, and it remained dead on the top of the tree, supported in a fork in such a manner that it would evidently not fall. I therefore returned home, and luckily found some Dyaks, who came back with me, and climbed up the tree for the animal. This was the first full-grown specimen I had obtained; but it was a female, and not nearly so large or remarkable as the full-grown males. It was, however, 3 ft. 6 in. high, and its arms stretched out to a width of 6 ft. 6 in. I preserved the skin of this specimen in a cask of arrack, and prepared a perfect skeleton, which was afterwards purchased for the Derby Museum.

Only four days afterwards some Dyaks saw another Mias near the same place, and came to tell me. We found it to be a rather large one, very high up on a tall tree. At the second shot it fell rolling over, but almost immediately got up again and began to climb. At a third shot it fell dead. This was also a full-grown female, and while preparing to carry it home, we found a young one face downwards in the bog. This little creature was only about a foot long, and had evidently been hanging to its mother when she first fell. Luckily it did not appear to have been wounded, and after we had cleaned the mud out of its mouth it began to cry out, and seemed quite strong and active. While carrying it home it got its hands in my beard, and grasped so tightly that I had great difficulty in getting free, for the fingers are habitually bent inwards at the last joint so as to form complete hooks. At this time it had not a single tooth, but a few days afterwards it cut its two lower front teeth. Unfortunately, I had no milk to give it, as neither Malays, Chinese nor Dyaks ever use the article, and I in vain inquired for any female animal that could suckle my little infant. I was therefore obliged to give it rice-water from a bottle with a quill in the cork, which after a few trials it learned to suck very well. This was very meagre diet, and the little creature did not thrive well on it, although I added sugar and cocoa-nut milk occasionally, to make it more nourishing. When I put my finger in its mouth it sucked with great vigour, drawing in its cheeks with all its might in the vain effort to extract some milk, and only after persevering a long time would it give up in disgust, and set up a scream very like that of a baby in similar circumstances.

When handled or nursed, it was very quiet and contented, but when laid down by itself would invariably cry; and for the first few nights was very restless and noisy. I fitted up a little box for a cradle, with a soft mat for it to lie upon, which was changed and washed everyday; and I soon found it necessary to wash the little Mias as well. After I had done so a few times, it came to like the operation, and as soon as it was dirty would begin crying and not leave off until I took it out and carried it to the spout, when it immediately became quiet, although it would wince a little at the first rush of the cold water and make ridiculously wry faces while the stream was running over its head. It enjoyed the wiping and rubbing dry amazingly, and when I brushed its hair seemed to be perfectly happy, lying quite still with its arms and legs stretched out while I thoroughly brushed the long hair of its back and arms. For the first few days it clung desperately with all four hands to whatever it could lay hold of, and I had to be careful to keep my beard out of its way, as its fingers clutched hold of hair more tenaciously than anything else, and it was impossible to free myself without assistance. When restless, it would struggle about with its hands up in the air trying to find something to take hold of, and, when it had got a bit of stick or rag in two or three of its hands, seemed quite happy. For want of something else, it would often seize its own feet, and after a time it would constantly cross its arms and grasp with each hand the long hair that grew just below the opposite shoulder. The great tenacity of its grasp soon diminished, and I was obliged to invent some means to give it exercise and strengthen its limbs. For this purpose I made a short ladder of three or four rounds, on which I put it to hang for a quarter of an hour at a time. At first it seemed much pleased, but it could not get all four hands in a comfortable position, and, after changing about several times, would leave hold of one hand after the other, and drop onto the floor. Sometimes when hanging only by two hands, it would loose one, and cross it to the opposite shoulder, grasping its own hair; and, as this seemed much more agreeable than the stick, it would then loose the other and tumble down, when it would cross both and lie on its back quite contentedly, never seeming to be hurt by its numerous tumbles. Finding it so fond of hair, I endeavoured to make an artificial mother, by wrapping up a piece of buffalo-skin into a bundle, and suspending it about a foot from the floor. At first this seemed to suit it admirably, as it could sprawl its legs about and always find some hair, which it grasped with the greatest tenacity. I was now in hopes that I had made the little orphan quite happy; and so it seemed for some time, until it began to remember its lost parent, and try to suck. It would pull itself up close to the skin, and try about everywhere for a likely place; but, as it only succeeded in getting mouthfuls of hair and wool, it would be greatly disgusted, and scream violently, and, after two or three attempts, let go altogether. One day it got some wool into its throat, and I thought it would have choked, but after much gasping it recovered, and I was obliged to take the imitation mother to pieces again, and give up this last attempt to exercise the little creature.

After the first week I found I could feed it better with a spoon, and give it a little more varied and more solid food. Well-soaked biscuit mixed with a little egg and sugar, and sometimes sweet potatoes, were readily eaten; and it was a never-failing amusement to observe the curious changes of countenance by which it would express its approval or dislike of what was given to it. The poor little thing would lick its lips, draw in its cheeks, and turn up its eyes with an expression of the most supreme satisfaction when it had a mouthful particularly to its taste. On the other hand, when its food was not sufficiently sweet or palatable, it would turn the mouthful about with its tongue for a moment as if trying to extract what flavour there was, and then push it all out between its lips. If the same food was continued, it would set up a scream and kick about violently, exactly like a baby in a passion.

After I had had the little Mias about three weeks, I fortunately obtained a young hare-lip monkey (Macacus cynomolgus), which, though small, was very active, and could feed itself. I placed it in the same box with the Mias, and they immediately became excellent friends, neither exhibiting the least fear of the other. The little monkey would sit upon the other's stomach, or even on its face, without the least regard to its feelings. While I was feeding the Mias, the monkey would sit by, picking up all that was spilt, and occasionally putting out its hands to intercept the spoon; and as soon as I had finished would pick off what was left sticking to the Mias' lips, and then pull open its mouth and see if any still remained inside; afterwards lying down on the poor creature's stomach as on a comfortable cushion. The little helpless Mias would submit to all these insults with the most exemplary patience, only too glad to have something warm near it, which it could clasp affectionately in its arms. It sometimes, however, had its revenge; for when the monkey wanted to go away, the Mias would hold on as long as it could by the loose skin of its back or head, or by its tail, and it was only after many vigorous jumps that the monkey could make his escape.

It was curious to observe the different actions of these two animals, which could not have differed much in age. The Mias, like a very young baby, lying on its back quite helpless, rolling lazily from side to side, stretching out all four hands into the air, wishing to grasp something, but hardly able to guide its fingers to any definite object; and when dissatisfied, opening wide its almost toothless mouth, and expressing its wants by a most infantine scream. The little monkey, on the other hand, in constant motion, running and jumping about wherever it pleased, examining everything around it, seizing hold of the smallest object with the greatest precision, balancing itself on the edge of the box or running up a post, and helping itself to anything eatable that came in its way. There could hardly be a greater contrast, and the baby Mias looked more baby-like by the comparison.

When I had had it about a month, it began to exhibit some signs of learning to run alone. When laid upon the floor it would push itself along by its legs, or roll itself over, and thus make an unwieldy progression. When lying in the box it would lift itself up to the edge into almost an erect position, and once or twice succeeded in tumbling out. When left dirty, or hungry, or otherwise neglected, it would scream violently until attended to, varied by a kind of coughing or pumping noise very similar to that which is made by the adult animal. If no one was in the house, or its cries were not attended to, it would be quiet after a little while, but the moment it heard a footstep would begin again harder than ever.

After five weeks it cut its two upper front teeth, but in all this time it had not grown the least bit, remaining both in size and weight the same as when I first procured it. This was no doubt owing to the want of milk or other equally nourishing food. Rice-water, rice, and biscuits were but a poor substitute, and the expressed milk of the cocoa-nut which I sometimes gave it did not quite agree with its stomach. To this I imputed an attack of diarrhoea from which the poor little creature suffered greatly, but a small dose of castor-oil operated well, and cured it. A week or two afterwards it was again taken ill, and this time more seriously. The symptoms were exactly those of intermittent fever, accompanied by watery swellings on the feet and head. It lost all appetite for its food, and, after lingering for a week a most pitiable object, died, after being in my possession nearly three months. I much regretted the loss of my little pet, which I had at one time looked forward to bringing up to years of maturity, and taking home to England. For several months it had afforded me daily amusement by its curious ways and the inimitably ludicrous expression of its little countenance. Its weight was three pounds nine ounces, its height fourteen inches, and the spread of its arms twenty-three inches. I preserved its skin and skeleton, and in doing so found that when it fell from the tree it must have broken an arm and a leg, which had, however, united so rapidly that I had only noticed the hard swellings on the limbs where the irregular junction of the bones had taken place.

Exactly a week after I had caught this interesting little animal, I succeeded in shooting a full-grown male Orangutan. I had just come home from an ento-mologising excursion when Charles [Charles Allen, an

English lad of sixteen, accompanied me as an assistant]
rushed in out of breath with running and excitement,
and exclaimed, interrupted by gasps, 'Get the gun, sir,
– be quick, – such a large Mias!' 'Where is it?' I asked,
taking hold of my gun as I spoke, which happened
luckily to have one barrel loaded with ball. 'Close by,
sir – on the path to the mines – he can't get away.'
Two Dyaks chanced to be in the house at the time, so
I called them to accompany me, and started off, telling
Charley to bring all the ammunition after me as soon
as possible. The path from our clearing to the mines
led along the side of the hill a little way up its slope,
and parallel with it at the foot a wide opening had been
made for a road, in which several Chinamen were
working, so that the animal could not escape into the
swampy forest below without descending to cross the
road or ascending to get round the clearings. We
walked cautiously along, not making the least noise,
and listening attentively for any sound which might
betray the presence of the Mias, stopping at intervals
to gaze upwards. Charley soon joined us at the place
where he had seen the creature, and having taken the
ammunition and put a bullet in the other barrel, we
dispersed a little, feeling sure that it must be somewhere near, as it had probably descended the hill, and
would not be likely to return again.

After a short time I heard a very slight rustling sound
overhead, but on gazing up could see nothing. I moved
about in every direction to get a full view into every
part of the tree under which I had been standing, when
I again heard the same noise but louder, and saw the

leaves shaking as if caused by the motion of some heavy animal which moved off to an adjoining tree. I immediately shouted for all of them to come up and try and get a view, so as to allow me to have a shot. This was not an easy matter, as the Mias had a knack of selecting places with dense foliage beneath. Very soon, however, one of the Dyaks called me and pointed upwards, and on looking I saw a great red hairy body and a huge black face gazing down from a great height, as if wanting to know what was making such a disturbance below. I instantly fired, and he made off at once, so that I could not then tell whether I had hit him.

He now moved very rapidly and very noiselessly for so large an animal, so I told the Dyaks to follow and keep him in sight while I loaded. The jungle was here full of large angular fragments of rock from the mountain above, and thick with hanging and twisted creepers. Running, climbing, and creeping among these, we came up with the creature on the top of a high tree near the road, where the Chinamen had discovered him, and were shouting their astonishment with open mouths: 'Ya Ya, Tuan; Orangutan, Tuan.' Seeing that he could not pass here without descending, he turned up again towards the hill, and I got two shots, and following quickly, had two more by the time he had again reached the path, but he was always more or less concealed by foliage, and protected by the large branch on which he was walking. Once while loading I had a splendid view of him, moving along a large limb of a tree in a semi-erect posture, and showing it to be an animal of the largest size. At the path he got on to one of the loftiest trees in the forest, and we could see one leg hanging down useless, having been broken by a ball. He now fixed himself in a fork, where he was hidden by thick foliage, and seemed disinclined to move. I was afraid he would remain and die in this position, and as it was nearly evening. I could not have got the tree cut down that day. I therefore fired again, and he then moved off, and going up the hill was obliged to get on to some lower trees, on the branches of one of which he fixed himself in such a position that he could not fall, and lay all in a heap as if dead, or dying.

I now wanted the Dyaks to go up and cut off the branch he was resting on, but they were afraid, saying he was not dead, and would come and attack them. We then shook the adjoining tree, pulled the hanging creepers, and did all we could to disturb him, but without effect, so I thought it best to send for two Chinamen with axes to cut down the tree. While the messenger was gone, however, one of the Dyaks took courage and climbed towards him, but the Mias did not wait for him to get near, moving off to another tree, where he got on to a dense mass of branches and creepers which almost completely hid him from our view. The tree was luckily a small one, so when the axes came we soon had it cut through; but it was so held up by jungle ropes and climbers to adjoining trees that it only fell into a sloping position. The Mias did not move, and I began to fear that after all we should not get him, as it was near evening, and half a dozen more trees would have to be cut down before the one he was on would fall. As a last resource we all began pulling at the creepers, which shook the tree very much, and, after a few minutes, when we had almost given up all hope, down he came with a crash and a thud like the fall of a giant. And he was a giant, his head and body being fully as large as a man's. He was of the kind called by the Dyaks 'Mias Chappan,' or 'Mias Pappan,' which has the skin of the face broadened out to a ridge or fold at each side. His outstretched arms measured seven feet three inches across, and his height, measuring fairly from the top of the head to the heel was four feet two inches. The body just below the arms was three feet two inches round, and was quite as long as a man's, the legs being exceedingly short in proportion. On examination we found he had been dreadfully wounded. Both legs were broken, one hip-joint and the root of the spine completely shattered, and two bullets were found flattened in his neck and jaws. Yet he was still alive when he fell. The two Chinamen carried him home tied to a pole, and I was occupied with Charley the whole of the next day preparing the skin and boiling the bones to make a perfect skeleton, which are now preserved in the Museum at Derby.

About ten days after this, on June 4th, some Dyaks came to tell us that the day before a Mias had nearly killed one of their companions. A few miles down the river there is a Dyak house, and the inhabitants saw a large Orang feeding on the young shoots of a palm by the riverside. On being alarmed he retreated towards the jungle which was close by, and a number of the men, armed with spears and choppers, ran out to intercept him. The man who was in front tried to run his spear through the animal's body, but the Mias seized it in his hands, and in an instant got hold of the man's arm, which he seized in his mouth, making his teeth meet in the flesh above the elbow, which he tore and lacerated in a dreadful manner. Had not the others been close behind, the man would have been more seriously injured, if not killed, as he was quite powerless; but they soon destroyed the creature with their spears and choppers. The man remained ill for a long time, and never fully recovered the use of his arm.

They told me the dead Mias was still lying where it had been killed, so I offered them a reward to bring it up to our landing-place immediately, which they promised to do. They did not come, however, until the next day, and then decomposition had commenced, and great patches of the hair came off, so that it was useless to skin it. This I regretted much, as it was a very fine full-grown male. I cut off the head and took it home to clean, while I got my men to make a closed fence about five feet high around the rest of the body, which would soon be devoured by maggots, small lizards, and ants, leaving me the skeleton. There was a great gash in his face, which had cut deep into the bone, but the skull was a very fine one, and the teeth were remarkably large and perfect.

On June 18th I had another great success, and obtained a fine adult male. A Chinaman told me he had seen him feeding by the side of the path to the river, and I found him at the same place as the first individual I had shot. He was feeding on an oval green fruit having a fine red arillus, like the mace which surrounds the nutmeg, and which alone he seemed to eat, biting off the thick outer rind and dropping it in a continual shower. I had found the same fruit in the stomach of some others which I had killed. Two shots caused this animal to loose his hold, but he hung for a considerable time by one hand, and then fell flat on his face and was half buried in the swamp. For several minutes he lay groaning and panting, while we stood close around, expecting every breath to be his last. Suddenly, however, by a violent effort he raised himself up, causing us all to step back a yard or two, when, standing nearly erect, he caught hold of a small tree, and began to ascend it. Another shot through the back caused him to fall down dead. A flattened bullet was found in his tongue, having entered the lower part of the abdomen and completely traversed the body, fracturing the first cervical vertebra. Yet it was after this fearful wound that he had risen, and begun climbing with considerable facility. This also was a full-grown male of almost exactly the same dimensions as the other two I had measured.

On June 21st I shot another adult female, which was eating fruit in a low tree, and was the only one which I ever killed by a single ball.

On June 24th I was called by a Chinaman to shoot a Mias, which, he said, was on a tree close by his house, at the coal-mines. Arriving at the place, we had some difficulty in finding the animal, as he had gone off into the jungle, which was very rocky and difficult to traverse. At last we found him up a very high tree, and could see that he was a male of the largest size. As soon as I had fired, he moved higher up the tree, and while he was doing so I fired again; and we then saw that one arm was broken. He had now reached the very highest part of an immense tree, and immediately began breaking off boughs all around, and laying them across and across to make a nest. It was very interesting to see how well he had chosen his place, and how rapidly he stretched out his unwounded arm in every direction, breaking off good-sized boughs with the greatest ease, and laying them back across each other, so that in a few minutes he had formed a compact mass of foliage, which entirely concealed him from our sight. He was evidently going to pass the night here, and would probably get away early the next morning, if not wounded too severely. I therefore fired again several times, in hopes of making him leave his nest; but, though I felt sure I had hit him, as at each shot he moved a little, he would not go away. At length he raised himself up, so that half his body was visible, and then gradually sank down, his head alone remaining on the edge of the nest. I now felt sure he was dead, and tried to persuade the Chinaman and his companion to cut down the tree; but it was a very large one, and they had been at work all day, and nothing would induce them to attempt it. The next morning, at daybreak, I came to the place, and found that the Mias was evidently dead, as his head was visible in exactly the same position as before. I now offered four Chinamen a day's wages each to cut the tree down at once, as a few hours of sunshine would cause decomposition on the surface of the skin; but, after looking at it and trying it, they determined that it was very big and very hard, and would not attempt it. Had I doubled my offer, they would probably have accepted it, as it would not have been more than two or three hours' work; and had I been on a short visit only, I would have done so; but as I was a resident, and intended remaining several months longer, it would not have answered to begin paying too exorbitantly, or I should have got nothing done in the future at a lower rate.

For some weeks after, a cloud of flies could be seen all day, hovering over the body of the dead Mias; but in about a month all was quiet, and the body was evidently drying up under the influence of a vertical sun alternating with tropical rains. Two or three months later two Malays, on the offer of a dollar, climbed the tree and let down the dried remains. The skin was almost entirely enclosing the skeleton, and inside were millions of the pupa-cases of flies and other insects, with thousands of two or three species of small necrophagous beetles. The skull had been much shattered by balls, but the skeleton was perfect, except one small wristbone, which had probably dropped out and been carried away by a lizard.

Three days after I had shot this one and lost it, Charles found three small Orangs feeding together. We had a long chase after them, and had a good opportunity of seeing how they make their way from tree to tree by always choosing those limbs whose branches are intermingled with those of some other tree, and then grasping several of the small twigs together before they venture to swing themselves across. Yet they do this so quickly and certainly, that they make way among the trees at the rate of full five or six miles an hour, as we had continually to run to keep up with them. One of these we shot and killed, but it remained high up in the fork of a tree; and, as young animals are of comparatively little interest, I did not have the tree cut down to get it.

At this time I had the misfortune to slip among some fallen trees, and hurt my ankle; and, not being careful enough at first, it became a severe inflamed ulcer, which would not heal, and kept me a prisoner in the house the whole of July and part of August. When I could get out again, I determined to take a trip up a branch of the Simunjon River to Semabang, where there was said to be a large Dyak house, a mountain with abundance of fruit, and plenty of Orangs and fine birds. As the river was very narrow, and I was obliged to go in a very small boat with little luggage, I only took with me a Chinese boy as a servant. I carried a cask of medicated arrack to put Mias skins in, and stores and ammunition for a fortnight. After a few miles, the stream became very narrow and winding, and the whole country on each side was flooded. On the banks were an abundance of monkeys – the common Macacus cynomolgus, a black Semnopithecus, and the extraordinary long-nosed monkey (Nasalis larvatus), which is as large as a three-year old child, has a very long tail, and a fleshy nose longer than that of the biggest-nosed man. The further we went on the narrower and more winding the stream became; fallen trees sometimes blocked up our passage, and sometimes tangled branches and creepers met completely across it, and had to be cut away before we could get on. It took us two days to reach Semabang, and we hardly saw a bit of dry land all the way. In the latter part of the journey I could touch the bushes on each side for miles; and we were often delayed by the screwpines (Pandanus), which grow abundantly in the water, falling across the stream. In other places dense rafts of floating grass completely filled up the channel, making our journey a constant succession of difficulties.

Near the landing-place we found a fine house, 250 feet long, raised high above the ground on posts, with a wide verandah and still wider platform of bamboo in front of it. Almost all the people, however, were away on some excursion after edible birds'-nests or bees'-wax, and there only remained in the house two or three old men and women with a lot of children. The mountain or hill was close by, covered with a complete forest of fruit-trees, among which the Durian and Mangusteen were very abundant; but the fruit was not yet quite ripe, except a little here and there. I spent a week at this place, going out everyday in various directions about the mountain, accompanied by a Malay, who had stayed with me while the other boatmen returned. For three days we found no Orangs, but shot a deer and several monkeys. On the fourth day, however, we found a Mias feeding on a very lofty Durian tree, and succeeded in killing it, after eight shots. Unfortunately it remained in the tree, hanging by its hands, and we were obliged to leave it and return home, as it was several miles off. As I felt pretty sure it would fall during the night, I returned to the place early the next morning, and found it on the ground beneath the tree. To my astonishment and pleasure, it appeared to be a different kind from any I had yet seen; for although a full-grown male, by its fully developed teeth and very large canines, it had no sign of the lateral protuberance on the face, and was about one-tenth smaller in all its dimensions than the other adult males. The upper incisors, however, appeared to be broader than in the larger species, a character distinguishing the Simia morio of Professor Owen, which he had described from the cranium of a female specimen. As it was too far to carry the animal home, I set to work and skinned the body on the spot, leaving the head, hands, and feet attached, to be finished at home. This specimen is now in the British Museum.

At the end of a week, finding no more Orangs, I returned home; and, taking in a few fresh stores, and this time accompanied by Charles, went up another branch of the river, very similar in character, to a place called Menyille, where there were several small Dyak houses and one large one. Here the landing place was a bridge of rickety poles, over a considerable distance of water; and I thought it safer to leave my cask of arrack securely placed in the fork of a tree. To prevent the natives from drinking it, I let several of them see me put in a number of snakes and lizards; but I rather think this did not prevent them from tasting it. We were accommodated here in the verandah of the large house, in which were several great baskets of dried human heads, the trophies of past generations of head-hunters. Here also there was a little mountain covered with fruit-trees, and there were some magnificent Durian trees close by the house, the fruit of which was ripe; and as the Dyaks looked upon me as a benefactor in killing the Mias, which destroys a great deal of their fruit, they let us eat as much as we liked; we revelled in this emperor of fruits in its greatest perfection.

The very day after my arrival in this place, I was so fortunate as to shoot another adult male of the small Orang, the Mias-kassir of the Dyaks. It fell when dead, but caught in a fork of the tree and remained fixed. As I was very anxious to get it, I tried to persuade two young Dyaks who were with me to cut down the tree, which was tall, perfectly straight and smooth-barked, and without a branch for fifty or sixty feet. To my surprise, they said they would prefer climbing up it, but it would be a good deal of trouble, and, after a little talking together, they said they would try. They first went to a clump of bamboo that stood near, and cut down one of the largest stems. From this they chopped off a short piece, and splitting it, made a couple of stout pegs, about a foot long and sharp at one end. Then cutting a thick piece of wood for a mallet, they drove one of the pegs into the tree and hung their weight upon it. It held, and this seemed to satisfy them, for they immediately began making a quantity of pegs of the same kind, while I looked on with great interest, wondering how they could possibly ascend such a lofty tree by merely driving pegs in it, the failure of any one of which at a good height would certainly cause their death. When about two dozen pegs were made, one of them began cutting some very long and slender bamboo from another clump, and also prepared some cord from the bark of a small tree. They now drove in a peg very firmly at about three feet from the ground, and bringing one of the long bamboos, stood it upright close to the tree, and bound it firmly to the two first pegs, by means of the bark cord and small notches near the head of each peg. One of the Dyaks now stood on the first peg and drove in a third, about level with his face, to which he tied the bamboo in the same way, and then mounted another step, standing on one foot, and holding by the bamboo at the peg immediately above him, while he drove in the next one. In this manner he ascended about twenty feet; when the upright bamboo was becoming thin, another was handed up by his companion, and this was joined by tying both bamboos to three or four of the pegs. When this was also nearly ended, a third was added, and shortly after, the lowest branches of the tree were reached, along which the young Dyak scrambled, and soon sent the Mias tumbling down headlong. I was exceedingly struck by the ingenuity of this mode of climbing, and the admirable manner in which the peculiar properties of the bamboo were made available. The ladder itself was perfectly safe, since if any one peg were loose or faulty, and gave way, the strain would be thrown on several others above and below it. I now understood the use of the line of bamboo pegs sticking in trees, which I had often seen, and wondered for what purpose they could have been put there. This animal was almost identical in size and appearance with the one I had obtained at Semabang, and was the only other male specimen of the Simia morio which I obtained. It is now in the Derby Museum.

I afterwards shot two adult females and two young ones of different ages, all of which I preserved. One of the females, with several young ones, was feeding on a Durian tree with unripe fruit; and as soon as she saw us she began breaking off branches and the great spiny fruits with every appearance of rage, causing such a shower of missiles as effectually kept us from approaching too near the tree. This habit of throwing down branches when irritated has been doubted, but I have, as here narrated, observed it myself on at least three separate occasions. It was however always the female Mias who behaved in this way, and it may be that the male, trusting more to his great strength and his powerful canine teeth, is not afraid of any other animal, and does not want to drive them away, while the parental instinct of the female leads her to adopt this mode of defending herself and her young ones.

In preparing the skins and skeletons of these animals, I was much troubled by the Dyak dogs, which, being always kept in a state of semi-starvation, are ravenous for animal food. I had a great iron pan, in which I boiled the bones to make skeletons, and at night I covered this over with boards, and put heavy stones upon it; but the dogs managed to remove these and carried away the greater part of one of my specimens.

On another occasion they gnawed away a good deal of the upper leather of my strong boots, and even ate a piece of my mosquito-curtain, where some lamp-oil had been spilt over it some weeks before.

On our return down the stream, we had the fortune to fall in with a very old male Mias, feeding on some low trees growing in the water. The country was flooded for a long distance, but so full of trees and stumps that the laden boat could not be got in among them, and if it could have been we should only have frightened the Mias away. I therefore got into the water, which was nearly up to my waist, and waded on until I was near enough for a shot. The difficulty then was to load my gun again, for I was so deep in the water that I could not hold the gun sloping enough to pour the powder in. I therefore had to search for a shallow place, and after several shots under these trying circumstances, I was delighted to see the monstrous animal roll over into the water. I now towed him after me to the stream, but the Malays objected to having the animal put into the boat, and he was so heavy that I could not do it without their help. I looked about for a place to skin him, but not a bit of dry ground was to be seen, until at last I found a clump of two or three old trees and stumps, between which a few feet of soil had collected just above the water, which was just large enough for us to drag the animal upon it. I first measured him, and found him to be by far the largest I had yet seen, for, though the standing height was the same as the others (4 feet 2 inches), the outstretched arms were 7 feet 9 inches, which was six inches more than the previous one, and the immense broad face was 13½ inches wide, whereas the widest I had hitherto seen was only 11½ inches. The girth of the body was 3 feet 7½ inches. I am inclined to believe, therefore, that the length and strength of the arms, and the width of the face continues increasing to a very great age, while the standing height, from the sole of the foot to the crown of the head, rarely if ever exceeds 4 feet 2 inches.

As this was the last Mias I shot, and the last time I saw an adult living animal, I will give a sketch of its general habits, and any other facts connected with it. The Orangutan is known to inhabit Sumatra and Borneo, and there is every reason to believe that it is confined to these two great islands, in the former of which, however, it seems to be much more rare. In Borneo it has a wide range, inhabiting many districts on the southwest, southeast, northeast, and northwest coasts, but appears to be chiefly confined to the low and swampy forests. It seems, at first sight, very inexplicable that the Mias should be quite unknown in the Sarawak valley, while it is abundant in Sambas, on the west, and Sadong, on the east. But when we know the habits and mode of life of the animal, we see a sufficient reason for this apparent anomaly in the physical features of the Sarawak district. In the Sadong, where I observed it, the Mias is only found when the country is low level and swampy, and at the same time covered with a lofty virgin forest. From these swamps rise many isolated mountains, on some of which the Dyaks have settled and covered with plantations of fruit trees.

These are a great attraction to the Mias, which comes to feed on the unripe fruits, but always retires to the swamp at night. Where the country becomes slightly elevated, and the soil dry, the Mias is no longer to be found. For example, in all the lower part of the Sadong valley it abounds, but as soon as we ascend above the limits of the tides, where the country, though still flat, is high enough to be dry, it disappears. Now the Sarawak valley has this peculiarity – the lower portion though swampy, is not covered with a continuous lofty forest, but is principally occupied by the Nipa palm; and near the town of Sarawak where the country becomes dry, it is greatly undulated in many parts, and covered with small patches of virgin forest, and much second-growth jungle on the ground, which has once been cultivated by the Malays or Dyaks.

Now it seems probable to me that a wide extent of unbroken and equally lofty virgin forest is necessary to the comfortable existence of these animals. Such forests form their open country, where they can roam in every direction with as much facility as the Indian on the prairie, or the Arab on the desert, passing from tree-top to tree-top without ever being obliged to descend upon the earth. The elevated and the drier districts are more frequented by man, more cut up by clearings and low second-growth jungle – not adapted to its peculiar mode of progression, and where it would therefore be more exposed to danger, and more frequently obliged to descend upon the earth. There is probably also a greater variety of fruit in the Mias district, the small mountains which rise like islands out of it serving as gardens or plantations of a sort, where the trees of the uplands are to be found in the very midst of the swampy plains.

It is a singular and very interesting sight to watch a Mias making his way leisurely through the forest. He walks deliberately along some of the larger branches in the semi-erect attitude which the great length of his arms and the shortness of his legs cause him naturally to assume; and the disproportion between these limbs is increased by his walking on his knuckles, not on the palm of the hand, as we should do. He seems always to choose those branches which intermingle with an adjoining tree, on approaching which he stretches out his long arms, and seizing the opposing boughs, grasps them together with both hands, seems to try their strength, and then deliberately swings himself across to the next branch, on which he walks along as before. He never jumps or springs, or even appears to hurry himself, and yet manages to get along almost as quickly as a person can run through the forest beneath. The long and powerful arms are of the greatest use to the animal, enabling it to climb easily up the loftiest trees, to seize fruits and young leaves from slender boughs which will not bear its weight, and to gather leaves and branches with which to form its nest. I have already described how it forms a nest when wounded, but it uses a similar one to sleep on almost every night. This is placed low down, however, on a small tree not more than from twenty to fifty feet from the ground, probably because it is warmer and less exposed to wind than higher up. Each Mias is said to make a fresh one for himself every night; but I should think that is hardly probable, or their remains would be much more abundant; for though I saw several about the coal-mines, there must have been many Orangs about every day, and in a year their deserted nests would become very numerous. The Dyaks say that, when it is very wet, the Mias covers himself over with leaves of pandanus, or large ferns, which has perhaps led to the story of his making a hut in the trees.

The Orang does not leave his bed until the sun has well risen and has dried up the dew upon the leaves. He feeds all through the middle of the day, but seldom returns to the same tree two days running. They do not seem much alarmed at man, as they often stared down upon me for several minutes, and then only moved away slowly to an adjacent tree. After seeing one, I have often had to go half a mile or more to fetch my gun, and in nearly every case have found it on the same tree, or within a hundred yards, when I returned. I never saw two full-grown animals together, but both males and females are sometimes accompanied by half-grown young ones, while, at other times, three or four young ones were seen in company. Their food consists almost exclusively of fruit, with occasionally leaves, buds, and young shoots. They seem to prefer unripe fruits, some of which were very sour, others intensely bitter, particularly the large red, fleshy arillus of one which seemed an especial favourite. In other cases they eat only the small seed of a large fruit, and they almost always waste and destroy more than they eat, so that there is a continual rain of rejected portions below the tree they are feeding on. The Durian is an especial favourite, and quantities of this delicious fruit are destroyed wherever it grows surrounded by forest, but they will not cross clearings to get at them. It seems wonderful how the animal can tear open this fruit, the outer covering of which is so thick and tough, and closely covered with strong conical spines. It probably bites off a few of these first, and then, making a small hole, tears open the fruit with its powerful fingers.

The Mias rarely descends to the ground, except when pressed by hunger, it seeks succulent shoots by the riverside; or, in very dry weather, has to search after water, of which it generally finds sufficient in the hollows of leaves. Only once I saw two half-grown Orangs on the ground in a dry hollow at the foot of the Simunjon hill. They were playing together, standing erect, and grasping each other by the arms. It may be safely stated, however, that the Orang never walks erect, unless when using its hands to support itself by branches overhead or when attacked. Representations of its walking with a stick are entirely imaginary.

The Dyaks all declare that the Mias is never attacked by any animal in the forest, with two rare exceptions; and the accounts I received of these are so curious that I give them nearly in the words of my informants, old Dyak chiefs, who had lived all their lives in the places where the animal is most abundant. The first of whom I inquired said: 'No animal is strong enough to hurt the Mias, and the only creature he ever fights with is the crocodile. When there is no fruit in the jungle, he goes to seek food on the banks of the river where there are plenty of young shoots that he likes, and fruits that grow close to the water. Then the crocodile sometimes tries to seize him, but the Mias gets upon him, and beats him with his hands and feet, and tears him and kills him.' He added that he had once seen such a fight, and that he believes that the Mias is always the victor.

My next informant was the Orang Kaya, or chief of the Balow Dyaks, on the Simunjon River. He said: 'The Mias has no enemies; no animals dare attack it but the crocodile and the python. He always kills the crocodile by main strength, standing upon it, pulling open its jaws, and ripping up its throat. If a python attacks a Mias, he seizes it with his hands, and then bites it, and soon kills it. The Mias is very strong; there is no animal in the jungle so strong as he.'

It is very remarkable that an animal so large, so peculiar, and of such a high type of form as the Orangutan, should be confined to so limited a district – to two islands, and those almost the last inhabited by the higher Mammalia; for, east of Borneo and Java, the Quadrumania, Ruminants, Carnivora, and many other groups of Mammalia diminish rapidly, and soon entirely disappear. When we consider, further, that almost all other animals have in earlier ages been represented by allied yet distinct forms – that, in the latter part of the tertiary period, Europe was inhabited by bears, deer, wolves, and cats; Australia by kangaroos and other marsupials; South America by gigantic sloths and ant-eaters; all different from any now existing, though intimately allied to them – we have every reason to believe that the Orangutan, the Chimpanzee, and the Gorilla have also had their forerunners. With what interest must every naturalist look forward to the time when the caves and tertiary deposits of the tropics may be thoroughly examined, and the past history and earliest appearance of the great man-like apes be made known at length.

[...]

Borneo: The Country of
the Hill Dyaks

As the wet season was approaching, I determined to return to Sarawak, sending all my collections with Charles Allen around by sea, while I myself proposed to go up to the sources of the Sadong River and descend by the Sarawak valley. As the route was somewhat difficult, I took the smallest quantity of baggage, and only one servant, a Malay lad named Bujon, who knew the language of the Sadong Dyaks, with whom he had traded. We left the mines on the 27th of November, and the next day reached the Malay village of Gúdong, where I stayed a short time to buy fruit and eggs, and called upon the Datu Bandar, or Malay governor of the place. He lived in a large, arid well-built house, very dirty outside and in, and was very inquisitive about my business, and particularly about the coal-mines. These puzzle the natives exceedingly, as they cannot understand the extensive and costly preparations for working coal, and cannot believe it is to be used only as fuel when wood is so abundant and so easily obtained. It was evident that Europeans seldom came here, for numbers of women skeltered away as I walked through the village and one girl about ten or twelve years old, who had just brought a bamboo full of water from the river, threw it down with a cry of horror and alarm the moment she caught sight of me, turned around and jumped into the stream. She swam beautifully, and kept looking back as if expecting I would follow her, screaming violently all the time; while a number of men and boys were laughing at her ignorant terror.

At Jahi, the next village, the stream became so swift in consequence of a flood, that my heavy boat could make no way, and I was obliged to send it back and go on in a very small open one. So far the river had been very monotonous, the banks being cultivated as rice-fields, and little thatched huts alone breaking the unpicturesque line of muddy bank crowned with tall grasses, and backed by the top of the forest behind the cultivated ground. A few hours beyond Jahi we passed the limits of cultivation, and had the beautiful virgin forest coming down to the water's edge, with its palms and creepers, its noble trees, its ferns, and epiphytes. The banks of the river were, however, still generally flooded, and we had some difficulty in finding a dry spot to sleep on. Early in the morning we reached Empugnan, a small Malay village, situated at the foot of an isolated mountain which had been visible from the mouth of the Simunjon River. Beyond here the tides are not felt, and we now entered upon a district of elevated forest, with a finer vegetation. Large trees stretch out their arms across the stream, and the steep, earthy banks are clothed with ferns and zingiberaceous plants.

Early in the afternoon we arrived at Tabókan, the first village of the Hill Dyaks. On an open space near the river, about twenty boys were playing at a game something like what we call 'prisoner's base;' their ornaments of beads and brass wire and their gay-coloured kerchiefs and waist-cloths showing to much advantage, and forming a very pleasing sight. On being called by Bujon, they immediately left their game to carry my things up to the 'headhouse,' – a circular building attached to most Dyak villages, and serving as a lodging for strangers, the place for trade, the sleeping-room of the unmarried youths, and the general council-chamber. It is elevated on lofty posts, has a large fireplace in the middle and windows in the roof all round, and forms a very pleasant and comfortable abode. In the evening it was crowded with young men and boys, who came to look at me. They were mostly fine young fellows, and I could not help admiring the simplicity and elegance of their costume. Their only dress is the long 'chawat,' or waist-cloth, which hangs down before and behind. It is generally of blue cotton, ending in three broad bands of red, blue, and white. Those who can afford it wear a handkerchief on the head, which is either red, with a narrow border of gold lace, or of three colours, like the 'chawat.' The large flat moon-shaped brass earrings, the heavy necklace of white or black beads, rows of brass rings on the arms and legs, and armlets of white shell, all serve to relieve and set off the pure reddish brown skin and jet-black hair. Add to this the little pouch containing materials for betel-chewing, and a long slender knife, both invariably worn at the side, and you have the everyday dress of the young Dyak gentleman.

The 'Orang Kaya,' or rich man, as the chief of the

tribe is called, now came in with several of the older men; and the 'bitchara' or talk commenced, about getting a boat and men to take me on the next morning. As I could not understand a word of their language, which is very different from Malay, I took no part in the proceedings, but was represented by my boy Bujon, who translated to me most of what was said. A Chinese trader was in the house, and he, too, wanted men the next day; but on his hinting this to the Orang Kaya, he was sternly told that a white man's business was now being discussed, and he must wait another day before his could be thought about.

After the 'bitchara' was over and the old chiefs gone, I asked the young men to play or dance, or amuse themselves in their accustomed way; and after some little hesitation they agreed to do so. They first had a trial of strength, two boys sitting opposite each other, foot being placed against foot, and a stout stick grasped by both their hands. Each then tried to throw himself back, so as to raise his adversary up from the ground, either by main strength or by a sudden effort. Then one of the men would try his strength against two or three of the boys; and afterwards they each grasped their own ankle with a hand, and while one stood as firm as he could, the other swung himself around on one leg, so as to strike the other's free leg, and try to overthrow him. When these games had been played all around with varying success, we had a novel kind of concert. Some placed a leg across the knee, and struck the fingers sharply on the ankle, others beat their arms against their sides like a cock when he is going to crow, this making a great variety of clapping sounds, while another with his hand under his armpit produced a deep trumpet note; and, as they all kept time very well, the effect was by no means unpleasing. This seemed quite a favourite amusement with them, and they kept it up with much spirit.

The next morning we started in a boat about thirty feet long, and only twenty-eight inches wide. The stream here suddenly changes its character. Hitherto, though swift, it had been deep and smooth, and confined by steep banks. Now it rushed and rippled over a pebbly, sandy, or rocky bed, occasionally forming miniature cascades and rapids, and throwing up on one side or the other broad banks of finely coloured pebbles. No paddling could make way here, but the Dyaks with bamboo poles propelled us along with great dexterity and swiftness, never losing their balance in such a narrow and unsteady vessel, though standing up and exerting all their force. It was a brilliant day, and the cheerful exertions of the men, the rushing of the sparkling waters, with the bright and varied foliage, which from either bank stretched over our heads, produced an exhilarating sensation which recalled my canoe voyages on the grander waters of South America.

Early in the afternoon we reached the village of Borotói, and, though it would have been easy to reach the next one before night, I was obliged to stay, as my men wanted to return and others could not possibly go on with me without the preliminary talking. Besides, a white man was too great a rarity to be allowed to escape them, and their wives would never have forgiven them if, when they returned from the fields, they found that such a curiosity had not been kept for them to see. On entering the house to which I was invited, a crowd of sixty or seventy men, women, and children gathered around me, and I sat for half an hour like some strange animal submitted for the first time to the gaze of an inquiring public. Brass rings were here in the greatest profusion, many of the women having their arms completely covered with them, as well as their legs from the ankle to the knee. Round the waist they wear a dozen or more coils of fine rattan stained red, to which the petticoat is attached. Below this are generally a number of coils of brass wire, a girdle of small silver coins, and sometimes a broad belt of brass ring armour. On their heads they wear a conical hat without a crown, formed of variously coloured beads, kept in shape by rings of rattan, and forming a fantastic but not unpicturesque headdress.

Walking out to a small hill near the village, cultivated as a rice-field, I had a fine view of the country, which was becoming quite hilly, and towards the south, mountainous. I took bearings and sketches of all that was visible, an operation which caused much astonishment to the Dyaks who accompanied me, and produced a request to exhibit the compass when I returned. I was then surrounded by a larger crowd than before, and when I took my evening meal in the midst of a circle of about a hundred spectators anxiously observing every movement and criticizing every mouthful, my thoughts involuntarily recurred to the lion at feeding time. Like those noble animals, I too was used to it, and it did not affect my appetite. The children here were more shy than at Tabókan, and I could not persuade them to play. I therefore turned showman myself, and exhibited the shadow of a dog's head eating, which pleased them so much that all the village in succession came out to see it. The 'rabbit on the wall' does not do in Borneo, as there is no animal it resembles. The boys had tops shaped something like whipping-tops, but spun with a string.

The next morning we proceeded as before, but the river had become so rapid and shallow and the boats were all so small, that though I had nothing with me but a change of clothes, a gun, and a few cooking utensils, two were required to take me on. The rock which appeared here and there on the riverbank was an indurated clay-slate, sometimes crystalline, and thrown up almost vertically. Right and left of us rose isolated limestone mountains, their white precipices glistening in the sun and contrasting beautifully with the luxuriant vegetation that elsewhere clothed them. The river bed was a mass of pebbles, mostly pure white quartz, but with abundance of jasper and agate, presenting a beautifully variegated appearance. It was only ten in the morning when we arrived at Budu, and, though there were plenty of people about, I could not induce them to allow me to go on to the next village. The Orang Kaya said that if I insisted on having men, of course he would get them, but when I took him at his word and said I must have them, there came a fresh remonstrance; and the idea of my going on that day seemed so painful that I was obliged to submit. I therefore walked out over the rice-fields, which are here very extensive, covering a number of the little hills and valleys into which the whole country seems broken up, and obtained a fine view of hills and mountains in every direction.

In the evening the Orang Kaya came in full dress (a spangled velvet jacket, but no trowsers), and invited me over to his house, where he gave me a seat of honour under a canopy of white calico and coloured handkerchiefs. The great verandah was crowded with people, and large plates of rice with cooked and fresh eggs were placed on the ground as presents for me. A very old man then dressed himself in bright-coloured cloths and many ornaments, and sitting at the door, murmured a long prayer or invocation, sprinkling rice from a basin he held in his hand, while several large gongs were loudly beaten and a salute of muskets fired off. A large jar of rice wine, very sour but with an agreeable flavour, was then handed around, and I asked to see some of their dances. These were, like most savage performances, very dull and ungraceful affairs; the men dressing themselves absurdly like women, and the girls making themselves as stiff and ridiculous as possible. All the time six or eight large Chinese gongs were being beaten by the vigorous arms of as many young men, producing such a deafening discord that I was glad to escape to the round house, where I slept very comfortably with half a dozen smoke-dried human skulls suspended over my head.

The river was now so shallow that boats could hardly get along. I therefore preferred walking to the next village, expecting to see something of the country, but was much disappointed, as the path lay almost entirely through dense bamboo thickets. The Dyaks get two crops off the ground in succession; one of rice, and the other of sugarcane, maize, and vegetables. The ground then lies fallow eight or ten years, and becomes covered with bamboos and shrubs, which often completely arch over the path and shut out everything from the view. Three hours walking brought us to the village of Senankan, where I was again obliged to remain the whole day, which I agreed to do on the promise of the Orang Kaya that his men should next day take me through two other villages across to Senna, at the head of the Sarawak River. I amused myself as I best could till evening, by walking about the high ground near, to get views of the country and bearings of the chief mountains. There was then another public audience, with gifts of rice and eggs, and drinking of rice wine. These Dyaks cultivate a great extent of ground, and supply a good deal of rice to Sarawak. They are rich in gongs, brass trays, wire, silver coins, and other articles in which a Dyak's wealth consists; and their women and children are all highly ornamented with bead necklaces, shells, and brass wire.

In the morning I waited some time, but the men that were to accompany me did not make their appearance. On sending to the Orang Kaya I found that both he and another head-man had gone out for the day, and on inquiring the reason was told that they could not persuade any of their men to go with me because the journey was a long and fatiguing one. As I was determined to get on, I told the few men that remained that the chiefs had behaved very badly, and that I should acquaint the Rajah with their conduct, and I wanted to start immediately. Every man present made some excuse, but others were sent for, and by hint of threats and promises, and the exertion of all Bujon's eloquence, we succeeded in getting off after two hours' delay.

For the first few miles our path lay over a country cleared for rice-fields, consisting entirely of small but deep and sharply-cut ridges and valleys without a yard of level ground. After crossing the Kayan river, a main branch of the Sadong, we got on to the lower slopes of the Seboran Mountain, and the path lay along a sharp and moderately steep ridge, affording an excellent view of the country. Its features were exactly those of the Himalayas in miniature, as they are described by Dr Hooker and other travellers, and looked like a natural model of some parts of those vast mountains on a scale of about a tenth – thousands of feet being here represented by hundreds. I now discovered the source of the beautiful pebbles which had so pleased me in the riverbed. The slatey rocks had ceased, and these mountains seemed to consist of a sandstone conglom-erate, which was in some places a mere mass of pebbles cemented together. I might have known that such small streams could not produce such vast quantities of well-rounded pebbles of the very hardest materials. They had evidently been formed in past ages, by the action of some continental stream or seabeach, before the great island of Borneo had risen from the ocean. The existence of such a system of hills and valleys reproducing in miniature all the features of a great mountain region, has an important bearing on the modern theory that the form of the ground is mainly due to atmospheric rather than to subterranean action. When we have a number of branching valleys and ravines running in many different directions within a square mile, it seems hardly possible to impute their formation, or even their orgination, to rents and fissures produced by earthquakes. On the other hand, the nature of the rock, so easily decomposed and removed by water, and the known action of the abundant tropical rains, are in this case, at least, quite sufficient causes for the production of such valleys. But the resemblance between their forms and outlines, their mode of divergence, and the slopes and ridges that divide them, and those of the grand mountain scenery of the Himalayas, is so remarkable, that we are forcibly led to the conclusion that the forces at work in the two cases have been the same, differing only in the time they have been in action, and the nature of the material they have had to work upon.

About noon we reached the village of Menyerry, beautifully situated on a spur of the mountain about 600 feet above the valley, and affording a delightful view of the mountains of this part of Borneo. I here got a sight of Penrissen Mountain, at the head of the Sarawak River, and one of the highest in the district, rising to about 6,000 feet above the sea. To the south the Rowan, and further off the Untowan Mountains in the Dutch territory appeared equally lofty. Descending from Menyerry we again crossed the Kayan, which bends round the spur, and ascended to the pass which divides the Sadong and Sarawak valleys, and which is about 2,000 feet high. The descent from this point was very fine. A stream, deep in a rocky gorge, rushed on each side of us, to one of which we gradually descended, passing over many lateral gullys and along the faces of some precipices by means of native bamboo bridges. Some of these were several hundred feet long and fifty or sixty high, a single smooth bamboo four inches diameter forming the only pathway, while a slender handrail of the same material was often so shaky that it could only be used as a guide rather than a support.

Late in the afternoon we reached Sodos, situated on a spur between two streams, but so surrounded by fruit trees that little could be seen of the country. The house was spacious, clean and comfortable, and the people very obliging. Many of the women and children had never seen a white man before, and were very sceptical as to my being the same colour all over, as my face. They begged me to show them my arms and body, and they were so kind and good-tempered that I felt bound to give them some satisfaction, so I turned up my trousers and let them see the colour of my leg, which they examined with great interest.

In the morning early we continued our descent along a fine valley, with mountains rising 2,000 or 3,000 feet in every direction. The little river rapidly increased in size until we reached Serma, when it had become a fine pebbly stream navigable for small canoes. Here again the upheaved slatey rock appeared, with the same dip and direction as in the Sadong River. On inquiring for a boat to take me down the stream, I was told that the Senna Dyaks, although living on the river-banks, never made or used boats. They were mountaineers who had only come down into the valley about twenty years before, and had not yet got into new habits. They are of the same tribe as the people of Menyerry and Sodos. They make good paths and bridges, and cultivate much mountain land, and thus give a more pleasing and civilized aspect to the country than where the people move about only in boats, and confine their cultivation to the banks of the streams.

After some trouble I hired a boat from a Malay trader, and found three Dyaks who had been several times with Malays to Sarawak, and thought they could manage it very well. They turned out very awkward, constantly running aground, striking against rocks, and losing their balance so as almost to upset themselves and the boat – offering a striking contrast to the skill of the Sea Dyaks. At length we came to a really dangerous rapid where boats were often swamped, and my men were afraid to pass it. Some Malays with a boatload of rice here overtook us, and after safely passing down kindly sent back one of their men to assist me. As it was, my Dyaks lost their balance in the critical part of the passage, and had they been alone would certainly have upset the boat. The river now became exceedingly picturesque, the ground on each side being partially cleared for ricefields, affording a good view of the country. Numerous little granaries were built high up in trees overhanging the river, and having a bamboo bridge sloping up to them from the bank; and here and there a bamboo suspension bridge crossed the stream, where overhanging trees favoured their construction.

I slept that night in the village of the Sebungow Dyaks, and the next day reached Sarawak, passing through a most beautiful country where limestone mountains with their fantastic forms and white precipices shot up on every side, draped and festooned with a luxuriant vegetation. The banks of the Sarawak River are everywhere covered with fruit trees, which supply the Dyaks with a great deal of their food. The Mangosteen, Lansat, Rambutan, Jack, Jambou, and Blimbing, are all abundant; but most abundant and most esteemed is the Durian, a fruit about which very little is known in England, but which both by natives and Europeans in the Malay Archipelago is reckoned superior to all others. The old traveller Linschott, writing in 1599, says: 'It is of such an excellent taste that it surpasses in flavour all the other fruits of the world, according to those who have tasted it.' And Doctor Paludanus adds: 'This fruit is of a hot and humid nature. To those not used to it, it seems at first to smell like rotten onions, but immediately when they have tasted it, they prefer it to all other food. The natives give it honourable titles, exalt it, and make verses on it.' When brought into a house the smell is often so offensive that some persons can never bear to taste it. This was my own case when I first tried it in Malacca, but in Borneo I found a ripe fruit on the ground, and, eating it out of doors, I at once became a confirmed Durian eater.

The Durian grows on a large and lofty forest tree,

somewhat resembling an elm in its general character, but with a more smooth and scaly bark. The fruit is round or slightly oval, about the size of a large cocoanut, of a green colour, and covered all over with short stout spines the bases of which touch each other, and are consequently somewhat hexagonal, while the points are very strong and sharp. It is so completely armed, that if the stalk is broken off it is a difficult matter to lift one from the ground. The outer rind is so thick and tough, that from whatever height it may fall it is never broken. From the base to the apex five very faint lines may be traced, over which the spines arch a little; these are the sutures of the carpels, and show where the fruit may be divided with a heavy knife and a strong hand. The five cells are satiny white within, and are each filled with an oval mass of cream-coloured pulp, imbedded in which are two or three seeds about the size of chestnuts. This pulp is the eatable part, and its consistency and flavour are indescribable. A rich butter-like custard highly flavoured with almonds gives the best general idea of it, but intermingled with it come wafts of flavour that call to mind cream-cheese, onion-sauce, brown sherry, and other incongruities. Then there is a rich glutinous smoothness in the pulp which nothing else possesses, but which adds to its delicacy. It is neither acid, nor sweet, nor juicy; yet one feels the want of more of these qualities, for it is perfect as it is. It produces no nausea or other bad effect, and the more you eat of it the less you feel inclined to stop. In fact to eat Durians is a new sensation, worth a voyage to the East to experience.

When the fruit is ripe it falls of itself, and the only way to eat Durians in perfection is to get them as they fall; and the smell is then less overpowering. When unripe, it makes a very good vegetable if cooked, and it is also eaten by the Dyaks raw. In a good fruit season large quantities are preserved salted, in jars and bamboos, and kept the year round, when it acquires a most disgusting odour to Europeans, but the Dyaks appreciate it highly as a relish with their rice. There are in the forest two varieties of wild Durians with much smaller fruits, one of them orange-coloured inside; and these are probably the origin of the large and fine Durians, which are never found wild. It would not, perhaps, be correct to say that the Durian is the best of all fruits, because it cannot supply the place of the subacid juicy kinds, such as the orange, grape, mango, and mangosteen, whose refreshing and cooling qualities are so wholesome and grateful; but as producing a food of the most exquisite flavour, it is unsurpassed. If I had to fix on two only, as representing the perfection of the two classes, I should certainly choose the Durian and the Orange as the king and queen of fruits.

The Durian is, however, sometimes dangerous. When the fruit begins to ripen it falls daily and almost hourly, and accidents not unfrequently happen to persons walking or working under the trees. When a Durian strikes a man in its fall, it produces a dreadful wound, the strong spines tearing open the flesh, while the blow itself is very heavy; but from this very circumstance death rarely ensues, the copious effusion of blood preventing the inflammation which might otherwise take place. A Dyak chief informed me that he had been struck down by a Durian falling on his head, which he thought would certainly have caused his death, yet he recovered in a very short time.

Poets and moralists, judging from our English trees and fruits, have thought that small fruits always grew on lofty trees, so that their fall should be harmless to man, while the large ones trailed on the ground. Two of the largest and heaviest fruits known, however, the Brazil-nut fruit (Bertholletia) and Durian, grow on lofty forest trees, from which they fall as soon as they are ripe, and often wound or kill the native inhabitants. From this we may learn two things: first, not to draw general conclusions from a very partial view of nature; and secondly, that trees and fruits, no less than the varied productions of the animal kingdom, do not appear to be organized with exclusive reference to the use and convenience of man.

During my many journeys in Borneo, and especially during my various residences among the Dyaks, I first came to appreciate the admirable qualities of the Bamboo. In those parts of South America which I had previously visited, these gigantic grasses were comparatively scarce; and where found but little used, their place being taken as to one class of uses by the great variety of Palms, and as to another by calabashes and gourds. Almost all tropical countries produce Bamboos, and wherever they are found in abundance the natives apply them to a variety of uses. Their strength, lightness, smoothness, straightness, roundness and hollowness, the facility and regularity with which they can be split, their many different sizes, the varying length of their joints, the ease with which they can be cut and with which holes can be made through them, their hardness outside, their freedom from any pronounced taste or smell, their great abundance, and the rapidity of their growth and increase, are all qualities which render them useful for a hundred different purposes, to serve which other materials would require much more labour and preparation. The Bamboo is one of the most wonderful and most beautiful productions of the tropics, and one of nature's most valuable gifts to uncivilized man.

The Dyak houses are all raised on posts, and are often two or three hundred feet long and forty or fifty wide. The floor is always formed of strips split from large Bamboos, so that each may be nearly flat and about three inches wide, and these are firmly tied down with rattan to the joists beneath. When well made, this is a delightful floor to walk upon barefooted, the rounded surfaces of the bamboo being very smooth and agreeable to the feet, while at the same time affording a firm hold. But, what is more important, they form with a mat over them an excellent bed, the elasticity of the Bamboo and its rounded surface being far superior to a more rigid and a flatter floor. Here we at once find a use for Bamboo which cannot be supplied so well by another material without a vast amount of labour – palms and other substitutes requiring much cutting and smoothing, and not being equally good when finished. When, however, a flat, close floor is required, excellent boards are made by splitting open large Bamboos on one side only, and flattening them out so as to form slabs eighteen inches wide and six feet long, with which some Dyaks floor their houses. These with constant rubbing of the feet and the smoke of years become dark and polished, like walnut or old oak, so that their real material can hardly be recognized. What labour is here saved to a savage whose only tools are an axe and a knife, and who, if he wants boards, must hew them out of the solid trunk of a tree, and must give days and weeks of labour to obtain a surface as smooth and beautiful as the Bamboo thus treated affords him. Again, if a temporary house is wanted, either by the native in his plantation or by the traveller in the forest, nothing is so convenient as the Bamboo, with which a house can be constructed with a quarter of the labour and time than if other materials are used.

As I have already mentioned, the Hill Dyaks in the interior of Sarawak make paths for long distances from village to village and to their cultivated grounds, in the course of which they have to cross many gullies and ravines, and even rivers; or sometimes, to avoid a long circuit, to carry the path along the face of a precipice. In all these cases the bridges they construct are of Bamboo, and so admirably adapted is the material for this purpose, that it seems doubtful whether they ever would have attempted such works if they had not possessed it. The Dyak bridge is simple but well designed. It consists merely of stout Bamboos crossing each other at the road-way like the letter X, and rising a few feet above it. At the crossing they are firmly bound together, and to a large Bamboo which lays upon them and forms the only pathway, with a slender and often very shaky one to serve as a handrail. When a river is to be crossed, an overhanging tree is chosen from which the bridge is partly suspended and partly supported by diagonal struts from the banks, so as to avoid placing posts in the stream itself, which would be liable to be carried away by floods. In carrying a path along the face of a precipice, trees and roots are made use of for suspension; struts arise from suitable notches or crevices in the rocks, and if these are not sufficient, immense Bamboos fifty or sixty feet long are fixed on the banks or on the branch of a tree below. These bridges are traversed daily by men and women carrying heavy loads, so that any insecurity is soon discovered, and, as the materials are close at hand, immediately repaired. When a path goes over very steep ground, and becomes slippery in very wet or very dry weather, the Bamboo is used in another way. Pieces are cut about a yard long, and opposite notches being made at each end, holes are formed through which pegs are driven, and firm and convenient steps are thus formed with the greatest ease and celerity. It is true that much of this will decay in one or two seasons, but it can be so quickly replaced as to make it more economical than using a harder and more durable wood.

One of the most striking uses to which Bamboo is applied by the Dyaks, is to assist them in climbing lofty trees by driving in pegs in the way I have already described at page 31. This method is constantly used in order to obtain wax, which is one of the most valuable products of the country. The honey-bee of Borneo very generally hangs its combs under the branches of the Tappan, a tree which towers above all others in the forest, and whose smooth cylindrical trunk often rises a hundred feet without a branch. The Dyaks climb these lofty trees at night, building up their Bamboo ladder as they go, and bringing down gigantic honey-combs. These furnish them with a delicious feast of honey and young bees, besides the wax, which they sell to traders, and with the proceeds buy the much-coveted brass wire, earrings, and bold-edged handkerchiefs with which they love to decorate themselves. In ascend-ing Durian and other fruit trees which branch at from thirty to fifty feet from the ground, I have seen them use the Bamboo pegs only, without the upright Bamboo which renders them so much more secure.

The outer rind of the Bamboo, split and shaved thin, is the strongest material for baskets; hen-coops, bird-cages, and conical fish-traps are very quickly made from a single joint, by splitting off the skin in narrow strips left attached to one end, while rings of the same material or of rattan are twisted in at regular distances. Water is brought to the houses by little aqueducts formed of large Bamboos split in half and supported on crossed sticks of various heights so as to give it a regular fall. Thin long-jointed Bamboos form the Dyaks' only water-vessels, and a dozen of them stand in the corner of every house. They are clean, light, and easily carried, and are in many ways superior to earthen vessels for the same purpose. They also make excellent cooking utensils; vegetables and rice can be boiled in them to perfection, and they are often used when travelling. Salted fruit or fish, sugar, vinegar, and honey are preserved in them instead of in jars or bottles. In a small Bamboo case, prettily carved and ornamented, the Dyak carries his sirih and lime for betel chewing, and his little long-bladed knife has a Bamboo sheath. His favourite pipe is a huge hubble-bubble, which he will construct in a few minutes by inserting a small piece of Bamboo for a bowl obliquely into a large cylinder about six inches from the bottom containing water, through which the smoke passes to a long slender Bamboo tube. There are many other small matters for which Bamboo is daily used, but enough has now been mentioned to show its value. In other parts of the Archipelago I have myself seen it applied to many new uses, and it is probable that my limited means of observation did not make me acquainted with one-half the ways in which it is serviceable to the Dyaks of Sarawak.

While upon the subject of plants I may here mention a few of the more striking vegetable productions of Borneo. The wonderful Pitcher-plants, forming the genus Nepenthes of botanists, here reach their greatest development. Every mountain-top abounds with them, running along the ground, or climbing over shrubs and stunted trees; their elegant pitchers hanging in every direction. Some of these are long and slender, resembling in form the beautiful Philippine lace-sponge (Euplectella), which has now become so common; others are broad and short. Their colours are green, variously tinted and mottled with red or purple. The finest yet known were obtained on the summit of Kini-balou, in North-west Borneo. One of the broad sort, Nepenthes rajah, will hold two quarts of water in its pitcher. Another, Nepenthes Edwardsiania, has a narrow pitcher twenty inches long; while the plant itself grows to a length of twenty feet.

Ferns are abundant, but are not so varied as on the volcanic mountains of Java; and Tree-ferns are neither so plentiful nor so large as on that island. They grow, however, quite down to the level of the sea, and are generally slender and graceful plants from eight to fifteen feet high. Without devoting much time to the search I collected fifty species of Ferns in Borneo, and I have no doubt a good botanist would have obtained twice the number. The interesting group of Orchids is very abundant, but, as is generally the case, nine-tenths of the species have small and inconspicuous flowers. Among the exceptions are the fine Coelogynes, whose large clusters of yellow flowers ornament the gloomiest forests, and that most extraordinary plant, Vanda Lowii, which last is particularly abundant near some hot springs at the foot of the Penin-jauh Mountain. It grows on the lower branches of trees, and its strange pendant flower-spires often hang down so as almost to reach the ground. These are generally six or eight feet long, bearing large and handsome flowers three inches across, and varying in colour from orange to red, with deep purple-red spots. I measured one spike, which reached the extraordinary length of nine feet eight inches, and bore thirty-six flowers, spirally arranged upon a slender thread-like stalk. Specimens grown in our English hot-houses have produced flower-spires of equal length, and with a much larger number of blossoms.

Flowers were scarce, as is usual in equatorial forests, and it was only at rare intervals that I met with anything striking. A few fine climbers were sometimes seen, especially a handsome crimson and yellow Aeschynanthus, and a fine leguminous plant with clusters of large Cassia-like flowers of a rich purple colour. Once I found a number of small Anonaceous trees of the genus Polyalthea, producing a most striking effect in the gloomy forest shades. They were about thirty feet high, and their slender trunks were covered with large star-like crimson flowers, which clustered over them like garlands, and resembled some artificial decoration more than a natural product.

The forests abound with gigantic trees with cylindrical, buttressed, or furrowed stems, while occasionally the traveller comes upon a wonderful fig-tree, whose trunk is itself a forest of stems and aerial roots. Still more rarely are found trees which appear to have begun growing in mid-air, and from the same point send out wide-spreading branches above and a complicated pyramid of roots descending for seventy or eighty feet to the ground below, and so spreading on every side, that one can stand in the very centre with the trunk of the tree immediately overhead. I believe that they originate as parasites, from seeds carried by birds and dropped in the fork of some lofty tree. Hence descend aerial roots, clasping and ultimately destroying the supporting tree, which is in time entirely replaced by the humble plant which was at first dependent upon it. Thus we have an actual struggle for life in the vegetable kingdom, not less fatal to the vanquished than the struggles among animals which we can so much more easily observe and understand. The advantage of quicker access to light and warmth and air, which is gained in one way by climbing plants, is here obtained by a forest tree, which has the means of starting in life at an elevation which others can only attain after many years of growth, and then only when the fall of some other tree has made room for them. Thus it is that in the warm and moist and equable climate of the tropics, each available station is seized upon and becomes the means of developing new forms of life especially adapted to occupy it.

[. . .]

Celebes: Bird and Insect Hunting; an Earthquake

I left Lombock on the 30th of August, and reached Macassar in three days. It was with great satisfaction that I stepped on a shore which I had been vainly trying to reach since February, and where I expected to meet with so much that was new and interesting.

The coast of this part of Celebes is low and flat, lined with trees and villages so as to conceal the interior, except at occasional openings which show a wide extent of bare and marshy rice-fields. A few hills of no great height were visible in the background; but owing to the perpetual haze over the land at this time of the year, I could nowhere discern the high central range of the peninsula, or the celebrated peak of Bontyne at its southern extremity. In the roadstead of Macassar there was a fine 42-gun frigate, the guardship of the place, as well as a small war steamer and three or four little cutters used for cruising after the pirates which infest these seas. There were also a few square-rigged trading-vessels, and twenty or thirty native praus of various sizes. I brought letters of introduction to a Dutch gentleman, Mr Mesman, and also to a Danish shopkeeper, who could both speak English and who promised to assist me in finding a place to stay, suitable for my pursuits. In the meantime, I went to a kind of clubhouse, in default of any hotel in the place.

Macassar was the first Dutch town I had visited, and I found it prettier and cleaner than any I had yet seen in the East. The Dutch have some admirable local regulations. All European houses must be kept well white-washed, and every person must, at four in the afternoon, water the road in front of his house. The streets are kept clear of refuse, and covered drains carry away all impurities into large open sewers, into which the tide is admitted at high-water and allowed to flow out when it has ebbed, carrying all the sewage with it into the sea. The town consists chiefly of one long narrow street along the seaside, devoted to business, and principally occupied by the Dutch and Chinese merchants' offices and warehouses, and the native shops or bazaars. This extends northwards for more than a mile, gradually merging into native houses often of a most miserable description, but made to have a neat appearance by being all built up exactly to the straight line of the street, and being generally backed by fruit trees. This street is usually thronged with a native population of Bugis and Macassar men, who wear cotton trousers about twelve inches long, covering only from the hip to half-way down the thigh, and the universal Malay sarong, of gay checked colours, worn around the waist or across the shoulders in a variety of ways. Parallel to this street run two short ones which form the old Dutch town, and are enclosed by gates. These consist of private houses, and at their southern end is the fort, the church, and a road at right angles to the beach, containing the houses of the Governor and of the principal officials. Beyond the fort, again along the beach, is another long street of native huts and many country-houses of the tradesmen and merchants. All around extend the flat rice-fields, now bare and dry and forbidding, covered with dusty stubble and weeds. A few months back these were a mass of verdure, and their barren appearance at this season offered a striking contrast to the perpetual crops on the same kind of country in Lombock and Bali, where the seasons are exactly similar, but where an elaborate system of irrigation produces the effect of a perpetual spring.

The day after my arrival I paid a visit of ceremony to the Governor, accompanied by my friend the Danish merchant, who spoke excellent English. His Excellency was very polite, and offered me every facility for travelling about the country and prosecuting my researches in natural history. We conversed in French, which all Dutch officials speak very well.

Finding it very inconvenient and expensive to stay in the town, I removed at the end of a week to a little bamboo house, kindly offered me by Mr Mesman. It was situated about two miles away, on a small coffee plantation and farm, and about a mile beyond Mr M's own country-house. It consisted of two rooms raised about seven feet above the ground, the lower part being partly open (and serving excellently to skin birds in) and partly used as a granary for rice. There was a kitchen and other outhouses, and several cottages nearby, occupied by men in Mr M's employ.

After being settled a few days in my new house, I found that no collections could be made without going much further into the country. The rice-fields for some miles around resembled English stubbles late in autumn, and were almost as unproductive of bird or insect life. There were several native villages scattered about, so embosomed in fruit trees that at a distance they looked like clumps or patches of forest. These were my only collecting places; but they produced a very limited number of species, and were soon exhausted. Before I could move to any more promising district it was necessary to obtain permission from the Rajah of Goa, whose territories approach to within two miles of the town of Macassar. I therefore presented myself at the Governor's office and requested a letter to the Rajah, to claim his protection, and permission to travel in his territories whenever I might wish to do so. This was immediately granted, and a special messenger was sent with me to carry the letter.

My friend Mr Mesman kindly lent me a horse, and accompanied me on my visit to the Rajah, with whom he was great friends. We found his Majesty seated out of doors, watching the erection of a new house. He was naked from the waist up, wearing only the usual short trousers and sarong. Two chairs were brought out for us, but all the chiefs and other natives were seated on the ground. The messenger, squatting down at the Rajah's feet, produced the letter, which was sewn up in a covering of yellow silk. It was handed to one of the chief officers, who ripped it open and returned it to the Rajah, who read it, and then showed it to Mr M, who both speaks and reads the Macassar language fluently, and who explained fully what I required.

Permission was immediately granted me to go where I liked in the territories of Goa, but the Rajah desired, that should I wish to stay any time at a place I would first give him notice, in order that he might send someone to see that no injury was done me. Some wine was then brought us, and afterwards some detestable coffee and wretched sweetmeats, for it is a fact that I have never tasted good coffee where people grow it themselves.

Although this was the height of the dry season, and there was a fine wind all day, it was by no means a healthy time of year. My boy Ali had hardly been a day on shore when he was attacked by fever, which put me to great inconvenience, as at the house where I was staying, nothing could be obtained but at mealtime. After having cured Ali, and with much difficulty got another servant to cook for me, I was no sooner settled at my country abode than the latter was attacked with the same disease; and, having a wife in the town, left me. Hardly was he gone than I fell ill myself with strong intermittent fever every other day. In about a week I got over it, by a liberal use of quinine, when scarcely was I on my legs than Ali again became worse than ever. Ali's fever attacked him daily, but early in the morning he was pretty well, and then managed to cook enough for me for the day. In a week I cured him, and also succeeded in getting another boy who could cook and shoot, and had no objection to go into the interior. His name was Baderoon, and as he was unmarried and had been used to a roving life, having been several voyages to North Australia to catch trepang or 'beche de mer', I was in hopes of being able to keep him. I also got hold of a little impudent rascal of twelve or fourteen, who could speak some Malay, to carry my gun or insect-net and make himself generally useful. Ali had by this time become a pretty good bird-skinner, so that I was fairly supplied with servants.

I made many excursions into the country, in search of a good station for collecting birds and insects. Some of the villages a few miles inland are scattered about in woody ground which has once been virgin forest, but of which the constituent trees have been for the most part replaced by fruit trees, and particularly by the large palm, Arenga saccharifera, from which wine and sugar are made, and which also produces a coarse black fibre used for cordage. That necessary of life, the bamboo, has also been abundantly planted. In such places I found a good many birds, among which were the fine cream-coloured pigeon, Carpophaga luctuosa, and the rare blue-headed roller, Coracias temmincki, which has a most discordant voice, and generally goes in pairs, flying from tree to tree, and exhibiting while at rest that all-in-a-heap appearance and jerking motion of the head and tail which are so characteristic of the great Fissirostral group to which it belongs. From this habit alone, the kingfishers, bee-eaters, rollers, trogons, and South American puff-birds, might be grouped together by a person who had observed them in a state of nature, but who had never had an opportunity of examining their form and structure in detail. Thousands of crows, rather smaller than our rook, keep up a constant cawing in these plantations;

the curious wood-swallows (Artami), which closely resemble swallows in their habits and flight but differ much in form and structure, twitter from the tree-tops; while a lyre-tailed drongo-shrike, with brilliant black plumage and milk-white eyes, continually deceives the naturalist by the variety of its unmelodious notes.

In the more shady parts butterflies were tolerably abundant; the most common being species of Euplaea and Danais, which frequent gardens and shrubberies, and owing to their weak flight are easily captured. A beautiful pale blue and black butterfly, which flutters along near the ground among the thickets, and settles occasionally upon flowers, was one of the most striking; and scarcely less so, was one with a rich orange band on a blackish ground – these both belong to the Pieridae, the group that contains our common white butterflies, although differing so much from them in appearance. Both were quite new to European naturalists. [The former has been named Eronia tritaea; the latter Tachyris ithonae.] Now and then I extended my walks some miles further, to the only patch of true forest I could find, accompanied by my two boys with guns and insect-net. We used to start early, taking our breakfast with us, and eating it wherever we could find shade and water. At such times my Macassar boys would put a minute fragment of rice and meat or fish on a leaf, and lay it on a stone or stump as an offering to the deity of the spot; for though nominal Mahometans the Macassar people retain many pagan superstitions, and are but lax in their religious observances. Pork, it is true, they hold in abhorrence, but will not refuse wine when offered them, and consume immense quantities of 'sagueir,' or palm-wine, which is about as intoxicating as ordinary beer or cider. When well made it is a very refreshing drink, and we often took a draught at some of the little sheds dignified by the name of bazaars, which are scattered about the country wherever there is any traffic.

One day Mr Mesman told me of a larger piece of forest where he sometimes went to shoot deer, but he assured me it was much further off, and that there were no birds. However, I resolved to explore it, and the next morning at five o'clock we started, carrying our breakfast and some other provisions with us, and intending to stay the night at a house on the borders of the wood. To my surprise two hours' hard walking brought us to this house, where we obtained permission to pass the night. We then walked on, Ali and Baderoon with a gun each, Paso carrying our provisions and my insect-box, while I took only my net and collecting-bottle and determined to devote myself wholly to the insects. Scarcely had I entered the forest when I found some beautiful little green and gold speckled weevils allied to the genus Pachyrhynchus, a group which is almost confined to the Philippine Islands, and is quite unknown in Borneo, Java, or Malacca. The road was shady and apparently much trodden by horses and cattle, and I quickly obtained some butterflies I had not before met with. Soon a couple of reports were heard, and coming up to my boys I found they had shot two specimens of one of the finest of known cuckoos, Phoenicophaus callirhynchus. This bird derives its name from its large bill being coloured of a brilliant yellow, red, and black, in about equal proportions. The tail is exceedingly long, and of a fine metallic purple, while the plumage of the body is light coffee brown. It is one of the characteristic birds of the island of Celebes, to which it is confined.

After sauntering along for a couple of hours we reached a small river, so deep that horses could only cross it by swimming, so we had to turn back; but as we were getting hungry, and the water of the almost stagnant river was too muddy to drink, we went towards a house a few hundred yards off. In the plantation we saw a small raised hut, which we thought would do well for us to breakfast in, so I entered, and found inside a young woman with an infant. She handed me a jug of water, but looked very much frightened. However, I sat down on the doorstep, and asked for the provisions. In handing them up, Baderoon saw the infant, and started back as if he had seen a serpent. It then immediately struck me that this was a hut in which, as among the Dyaks of Borneo and many other savage tribes, the women are secluded for some time after the birth of their child, and that we did very wrong to enter it; so we walked off and asked permission to eat our breakfast in the family mansion close at hand, which was of course granted. While I ate, three men, two women, and four children watched every motion, and never took eyes off me until I had finished.

On our way back in the heat of the day, I had the good fortune to capture three specimens of a fine Ornithoptera, the largest, the most perfect, and the most beautiful of butterflies. I trembled with excitement as I took the first out of my net and found it to be in perfect condition. The ground colour of this superb insect was a rich shining bronzy black, the lower wings delicately grained with white, and bordered by a row of large spots of the most brilliant satiny yellow. The body was marked with shaded spots of white, yellow, and fiery orange, while the head and thorax were intense black. On the under-side the lower wings were satiny white, with the marginal spots half black and half yellow. I gazed upon my prize with extreme interest, as I at first thought it was quite a new species. It proved however to be a variety of Ornithoptera remus, one of the rarest and most remarkable species of this highly esteemed group. I also obtained several other new and pretty butterflies. When we arrived at our lodging-house, being particularly anxious about my insect treasures, I suspended the box from a bamboo on which I could detect no sign of ants, and then began skinning some of my birds. During my work I often glanced at my precious box to see that no intruders had arrived, until after a longer spell of work than usual I looked again, and saw to my horror that a column of small red ants were descending the string and entering the box. They were already busy at work at the bodies of my treasures, and another half-hour would have seen my whole day's collection destroyed. As it was, I had to take every insect out, clean them thoroughly as well as the box, and then seek a place of safety for them. As the only effectual one, I begged a plate and a basin from my host, filled the former with water, and standing the latter in it placed my box on the top, and then felt secure for the night; a few inches of clean water or oil being the only barrier these terrible pests are not able to pass.

[...]

The rare and beautiful Butterflies of Celebes were the chief object of my search, and I found many species altogether new to me, but they were generally so active and shy as to render their capture a matter of great difficulty. Almost the only good place for them was in the dry beds of the streams in the forest, where, at damp places, muddy pools, or even on the dry rocks, all sorts of insects could be found. In these rocky forests dwell some of the finest butterflies in the world. Three species of Ornithoptera, measuring seven or eight inches across the wings, and beautifully marked with spots or masses of satiny yellow on a black ground, wheel through the thickets with a strong sailing flight. About the damp places are swarms of the beautiful blue-banded Papilios, miletus and telephus, the superb golden green P. macedon, and the rare little swallow-tail Papilio rhesus, all of which, though very active, I succeeded in capturing fine series of specimens.

I have rarely enjoyed myself more than during my residence here. As I sat taking my coffee at six in the morning, rare birds would often be seen on some tree close by, when I would hastily sally out in my slippers, and perhaps secure a prize I had been seeking after for weeks. The great hornbills of Celebes (Buceros cassidix) would often come with loud-flapping wings, and perch upon a lofty tree just in front of me; and the black baboon-monkeys, Cynopithecus nigrescens, often stared down in astonishment at such an intrusion into their domains while at night herds of wild pigs roamed about the house, devouring refuse, and obliging us to put away everything eatable or breakable from our little cooking-house. A few minutes' search on the fallen trees around my house at sunrise and sunset, would often produce me more beetles than I would meet with in a day's collecting, and odd moments could be made valuable which when living in villages or at a distance from the forest are inevitably wasted. Where the sugar-palms were dripping with sap, flies congregated in immense numbers, and it was by spending half an hour at these when I had the time to spare, that I obtained the finest and most remarkable collection of this group of insects that I have ever made.

Then what delightful hours I passed wandering up and down the dry river-courses, full of water-holes and rocks and fallen trees, and overshadowed by magnificent vegetation. I soon got to know every hole and rock and stump, and came up to each with cautious step and bated breath to see what treasures it would produce. At one place I would find a little crowd of the rare butterfly Tachyris zarinda, which would rise up at my approach, and display their vivid orange and cinnabar-red wings, while among them would flutter a few of the fine blue-banded Papilios. Where leafy branches hung over the gully, I might expect to find a grand Ornithoptera at rest and an easy prey. At certain rotten trunks I was sure to get the curious little tiger beetle, Therates flavilabris. In the denser thickets I would capture the small metal-blue butterflies (Amblypodia) sitting on the leaves, as well as some rare and beautiful leaf-beetles of the families Hispidae and Chrysomelidae.

I found that the rotten jack-fruits were very attractive to many beetles, and used to split them partly open and lay them about in the forest near my house to rot. A morning's search at these often produced me a score of species – Staphylinidae, Nitidulidae, Onthophagi, and minute Carabidae, being the most abundant. Now and then the 'sagueir' makers brought me a fine rose-chafer (Sternoplus schaumii) which they found licking up the sweet sap. Almost the only new birds I met with for some time were a handsome ground thrush (Pitta celebensis), and a beautiful violet-crowned dove (Ptilonopus celebensis), both very similar to birds I had recently obtained at Aru, but of distinct species.

[. . .]

During my stay at Rurukan, my curiosity was satisfied by experiencing a pretty sharp earthquake-shock. On the evening of June 29th, at a quarter after eight, as I was sitting reading, the house began shaking with a very gentle, but rapidly increasing motion. I sat still enjoying the novel sensation for some seconds; but in less than half a minute it became strong enough to shake me in my chair, and to make the house visibly rock about, and creak and crack as if it would fall to pieces. Then began a cry throughout the village of 'Tana goyang! tana goyang! (Earthquake! earthquake!)' Everybody rushed out of their houses – women screamed and children cried – and I thought it prudent to go out too. On getting up, I found my head giddy and my steps unsteady, and could hardly walk without falling. The shock continued about a minute, during which time I felt as if I had been turned round and round, and was almost seasick. Going into the house again, I found a lamp and a bottle of arrack upset. The tumbler which formed the lamp had been thrown out of the saucer in which it had stood. The shock appeared to be nearly vertical, rapid, vibratory, and jerking. It was sufficient, I have no doubt, to have thrown down brick, chimneys, walls, and church towers; but as the houses here are all low, and strongly framed of timber, it is impossible for them to be much injured, except by a shock that would utterly destroy a European city. The people told me it was ten years since they had had a stronger shock than this, at which time many houses were thrown down and some people killed.

At intervals of ten minutes to half an hour, slight shocks and tremors were felt, sometimes strong enough to send us all out again. There was a strange mixture of the terrible and the ludicrous in our situation. We might at any moment have a much stronger shock, which would bring down the house over us, or – what I feared more – cause a landslip, and send us down into the deep ravine on the very edge of which the village is built; yet I could not help laughing each time we ran out at a slight shock, and then in a few moments ran in again. The sublime and the ridiculous were here literally but a step apart. On the one hand, the most terrible and destructive of natural phenomena was in action around us – the rocks, the mountains, the solid earth were trembling and convulsed, and we were utterly impotent to guard against the danger that might at any moment overwhelm us. On the other hand was the spectacle of a number of men, women, and children running in and out of their houses, on what each time proved a very unnecessary alarm, as each shock ceased just as it became strong enough to frighten us. It seemed really very much like 'playing at earthquakes,' and made many of the people join me in a hearty laugh, even while reminding each other that it really might be no laughing matter.

At length the evening got very cold, and I became very sleepy, and determined to turn in; leaving orders to my boys, who slept nearer the door, to wake me in case the house was in danger of falling. But I miscalculated my apathy, for I could not sleep much. The shocks continued at intervals of half an hour or an hour all night, just strong enough to wake me thoroughly each time and keep me on the alert, ready to jump up in case of danger. I was therefore very glad when morning came. Most of the inhabitants had not been to bed at all, and some had stayed out of doors all night. For the next two days and nights shocks still continued at short intervals, and several times a day for a week, showing that there was some very extensive disturbance beneath our portion of the earth's crust. How vast the forces at work really are can only be properly appreciated when, after feeling their effects, we look abroad over the wide expanse of hill and valley, plain and mountain, and thus realize in a slight degree the immense mass of matter heaved and shaken. The sensation produced by an earthquake is never to be forgotten. We feel ourselves in the grasp of a power to which the wildest fury of the winds and waves are as nothing; yet the effect is more a thrill of awe than the terror which the more boisterous war of the elements produces. There is a mystery and an uncertainty as to the amount of danger we incur, which gives greater play to the imagination, and to the influences of hope and fear. These remarks apply only to a moderate earthquake. A severe one is the most destructive and the most horrible catastrophe to which human beings can be exposed.

Celebes: The Ship to the Aru Islands

It was the beginning of December, and the rainy season at Macassar had just set in. For nearly three months I had beheld the sun rise daily above the palm-groves, mount to the zenith, and descend like a globe of fire into the ocean, unobscured for a single moment of his course. Now dark leaden clouds had gathered over the whole heavens, and seemed to have rendered him permanently invisible. The strong east winds, warm and dry and dust-laden, which had hitherto blown as certainly as the sun had risen, were now replaced by variable gusty breezes and heavy rains, often continuous for three days and nights together; and the parched and fissured rice stubbles which during the dry weather had extended in every direction for miles around the town, were already so flooded as to be only passable by boats, or by means of a labyrinth of paths on the top of the narrow banks which divided the separate properties.

Five months of this kind of weather might be expected in Southern Celebes, and I therefore determined to seek some more favourable climate for collecting in during that period, and to return in the next dry season to complete my exploration of the district. Fortunately for me I was in one of the great emporiums of the native trade of the archipelago. Rattans from

Borneo, sandal-wood and bees'-wax from Flores and Timor, tripang from the Gulf of Carpentaria, cajputi-oil from Bouru, wild nutmegs and mussoi-bark from New Guinea, are all to be found in the stores of the Chinese and Bugis merchants of Macassar, along with the rice and coffee which are the chief products of the surrounding country. More important than all these however is the trade to Aru, a group of islands situated on the south-west coast of New Guinea, and of which almost the whole produce comes to Macassar in native vessels. These islands are quite out of the track of all European trade, and are inhabited only by black mop-headed savages, who yet contribute to the luxuri-ous tastes of the most civilized races. Pearls, mother-of-pearl, and tortoiseshell find their way to Europe, while edible birds' nests and 'tripang' or sea-slug are obtained by shiploads for the gastronomic enjoyment of the Chinese.

The trade to these islands has existed from very early times, and it is from them that Birds of Paradise, of the two kinds known to Linnaeus were first brought. The native vessels can only make the voyage once a year, owing to the monsoons. They leave Macassar in December or January at the beginning of the west monsoon, and return in July or August with the full strength of the east monsoon. Even by the Macassar people themselves, the voyage to the Aru Islands is looked upon as a rather wild and romantic expedition, full of novel sights and strange adventures. He who has made it is looked up to as an authority, and it remains with many the unachieved ambition of their lives. I myself had hoped rather than expected ever to reach this 'Ultima Thule' of the East: and when I found that I really could do so now, had I but courage to trust myself for a thousand miles' voyage in a Bugis prau, and for six or seven months among lawless traders and ferocious savages, I felt somewhat as I did when, a schoolboy, I was for the first time allowed to travel outside the stage-coach, to visit that scene of all that is strange and new and wonderful to young imaginations– London!

By the help of some kind friends I was introduced to the owner of one of the large praus which was to sail in a few days. He was a Javanese half-caste, intelligent, mild, and gentlemanly in his manners, and had a young and pretty Dutch wife, whom he was going to leave behind during his absence. When we talked about passage money he would fix no sum, but insisted on leaving it entirely to me to pay on my return exactly what I liked. 'And then,' said he, 'whether you give me one dollar or a hundred, I shall be satisfied, and shall ask no more.'

The remainder of my stay was fully occupied in laying in stores, engaging servants, and making every other preparation for an absence of seven months from even the outskirts of civilization. On the morning of December 13th, when we went on board at daybreak, it was raining hard. We set sail and it came on to blow. Our boat was lost astern, our sails damaged, and the evening found us back again in Macassar harbour. We remained there four days longer, owing to its raining all the time, thus rendering it impossible to dry and repair the huge mat sails. All these dreary days I remained on board, and during the rare intervals when it didn't rain, made myself acquainted with our outlandish craft, some of the peculiarities of which I will now endeavour to describe.

It was a vessel of about seventy tons burthen, and shaped something like a Chinese junk. The deck sloped considerably downward to the bows, which are thus the lowest part of the ship. There were two large rudders, but instead of being planed astern they were hung on the quarters from strong cross beams, which projected out two or three feet on each side, and to which extent the deck overhung the sides of the vessel amidships. The rudders were not hinged but hung with slings of rattan, the friction of which keeps them in any position in which they are placed, and thus perhaps facilitates steering. The tillers were not on deck, but entered the vessel through two square openings into a lower or half deck about three feet high, in which sit the two steersmen. In the after part of the vessel was a low poop, about three and a half feet high, which forms the captain's cabin, its furniture consisting of boxes, mats, and pillows. In front of the poop and mainmast was a little thatched house on deck, about four feet high to the ridge; and one compartment of this, forming a cabin six and half feet long by five and a half wide, I had all to myself, and it was the snuggest and most comfortable little place I ever enjoyed at sea. It was entered by a low sliding door of thatch on one side, and had a very small window on the other. The floor was of split bamboo, pleasantly elastic, raised six inches above the deck, so as to be quite dry. It was covered with fine cane mats, for the manufacture of which Macassar is celebrated; against the further wall were arranged my guncase, insect-boxes, clothes, and books; my mattress occupied the middle, and next the door were my canteen, lamp, and little store of luxuries for the voyage; while guns, revolver, and hunting knife hung conveniently from the roof. During these four miserable days I was quite jolly in this little snuggery more so than I should have been if confined the same time to the gilded and uncomfortable saloon of a first-class steamer. Then, how comparatively sweet was everything on board – no paint, no tar, no new rope, (vilest of smells to the qualmish!) no grease, or oil, or varnish; but instead of these, bamboo and rattan, and coir rope and palm thatch; pure vegetable fibres, which smell pleasantly if they smell at all, and recall quiet scenes in the green and shady forest.

Our ship had two masts, if masts they can be called, which were great moveable triangles. If in an ordinary ship you replace the shrouds and backstay by strong timbers, and take away the mast altogether, you have the arrangement adopted on board a prau. Above my cabin, and resting on cross-beams attached to the masts, was a wilderness of yards and spars, mostly formed of bamboo. The mainyard, an immense affair nearly a hundred feet long, was formed of many pieces of wood and bamboo bound together with rattans in an ingenious manner. The sail carried by this was of an oblong shape, and was hung out of the centre, so that when the short end was hauled down on deck the long end mounted high in the air, making up for the lowness of the mast itself. The foresail was of the same shape, but smaller. Both these were of matting, and, with two jibs and a fore and aft sail astern of cotton canvas, completed our rig.

The crew consisted of about thirty men, natives of Macassar and the adjacent coasts and islands. They were mostly young, and were short, broad-faced, good-humoured looking fellows. Their dress consisted gen-erally of a pair of trousers only, when at work, and a handkerchief twisted round the head, to which in the evening they would add a thin cotton jacket. Four of the elder men were 'jurumudis,' or steersmen, who had to squat (two at a time) in the little steerage before described, changing every six hours. Then there was an old man, the 'juragan,' or captain, but who was really what we should call the first mate; he occupied the other half of the little house on deck. There were about ten respectable men, Chinese or Bugis, whom our owner used to call 'his own people.' He treated them very well, shared his meals with them, and spoke to them always with perfect politeness; yet they were most of them a kind of slave debtors, bound over by the police magistrate to work for him at mere nominal wages for a term of years till their debts were liquidated. This is a Dutch institution in this part of the world, and seems to work well. It is a great boon to traders, who can do nothing in these thinly-populated regions without trusting goods to agents and petty dealers, who frequently squander them away in gambling and debauchery. The lower classes are almost all in a chronic state of debt. The merchant trusts them again and again, till the amount is something serious, when he brings them to court and has their services allotted to him for its liquidation. The debtors seem to think this no disgrace, but rather enjoy their freedom from responsibility, and the dignity of their position under a wealthy and well-known merchant. They trade a little on their own account, and both parties seem to get on very well together. The plan seems a more sensible one than that which we adopt, of effectually preventing a man from earning anything towards paying his debts by shutting him up in a jail.

My own servants were three in number. Ali, the Malay boy whom I had picked up in Borneo, was my head man. He had already been with me a year, could turn his hand to anything, and was quite attentive and trustworthy. He was a good shot, and fond of shooting, and I had taught him to skin birds very well. The second, named Baderoon, was a Macassar lad; also a pretty good boy, but a desperate gambler. Under pretence of buying a house for his mother, and clothes, for himself, he had received four months' wages about a week before we sailed, and in a day or two gambled away every dollar of it. He had come on board with no clothes, no betel, or tobacco, or salt fish, all which necessary articles I was obliged to send Ali to buy for him. These two lads were about sixteen, I should suppose; the third was younger, a sharp little rascal named Baso, who had been with me a month or two, and had learnt to cook tolerably. He was to fulfil the important office of cook and housekeeper, for I could not get any regular servants to go to such a terribly remote country; one might as well ask a chef de cuisine to go to Patagonia.

On the fifth day that I had spent on board (Dec. 15th) the rain ceased, and final preparations were made for starting. Sails were dried and furled, boats were constantly coming and going, and stores for the voyage, fruit, vegetables, fish, and palm sugar, were taken on board. In the afternoon two women arrived with a large party of friends and relations, and at parting there was a general noserubbing (the Malay kiss), and some tears shed. These were promising symptoms for our getting off the next day; and accordingly, at three in the morning, the owner came on board, the anchor was immediately weighed, and by four we set sail. Just as we were fairly off and clear of the other praus, the old juragan repeated some prayers, all around responding with 'Allah il Allah,' and a few strokes on a gong as an accompaniment, concluding with all wishing each other 'Salaamat jalan,' a safe and happy journey. We had a light breeze, a calm sea, and a fine morning, a prosperous commencement of our voyage of about a thousand miles to the far-famed Aru Islands.

Wallace's voyage took him through the Moluccas, stopping in the Ke (Kai) Islands before eventually reaching Dobbo (Dobo), the chief port of the Aru Islands, located on the small island of Wamma (Wamar). After a stay there he moved to the main island, then known as Aru but now known as Tanahbesar, settling for a prolonged period in the inland village of Wanumbai.

The Aru Islands: The Great Bird of Paradise; Life in an Inland Village

All the men and boys of Aru are expert archers, never stirring without their bows and arrows. They shoot all sorts of birds, as well as pigs and kangaroos occasionally, and thus have a tolerably good supply of meat to eat with their vegetables. The result of this better living is superior healthiness, well-made bodies, and generally clear skins. They brought me numbers of small birds in exchange for beads or tobacco, but mauled them terribly, notwithstanding my repeated instructions. When they got a bird alive they would often tie a string to its leg, and keep it a day or two, till its plumage was so draggled and dirtied as to be almost worthless. One of the first things I got from there was a living specimen of the curious and beautiful racquet-tailed kingfisher. Seeing how much I admired it, they afterwards brought me several more, which were all caught before daybreak, sleeping in cavities of the rocky banks of the stream. My hunters also shot a few specimens, and almost all of them had the red bill more or less clogged with mud and earth. This indicates the habits of the bird, which, though popularly [known as] a king-fisher, never catches fish, but lives on insects and minute shells, which it picks up in the forest, darting down upon them from its perch on some low branch. The genus Tanysiptera, to which this bird belongs, is remarkable for the enormously lengthened tail, which in all other kingfishers is small and short. Linnaeus named the species known to him 'the goddess kingfisher' (Alcedo dea), from its extreme grace and beauty, the plumage being brilliant blue and white, with the bill red, like coral. Several species of these interesting birds are now known, all confined within the very limited area which comprises the Moluccas, New Guinea, and the extreme North of Australia. They resemble each other so closely that several of them can only be distinguished by careful comparison. One of the rarest, however, which inhabits New Guinea, is very distinct from the rest, being bright red beneath instead of white. That which I now obtained was a new one, and has been named Tanysiptera hydrocharis, but in general form and coloration it is exactly similar to the larger species found in Amboyna.

New and interesting birds were continually brought in, either by my own boys or by the natives, and at the end of a week Ali arrived triumphant one afternoon with a fine specimen of the Great Bird of Paradise. The ornamental plumes had not yet attained their full growth, but the richness of their glossy orange colouring, and the exquisite delicacy of the loosely waving feathers, were unsurpassable. At the same time a great black cockatoo was brought in, as well as a fine fruit-pigeon and several small birds, so that we were all kept hard at work skinning till sunset. Just as we had cleared away and packed up for the night, a strange beast was brought, which had been shot by the natives. It resembled in size, and in its white woolly covering, a small fat lamb, but had short legs, hand-like feet with large claws, and a long prehensile tail. It was a Cuscus (C. maculatus), one of the curious marsupial animals of the Papuan region, and I was very desirous to obtain the skin. The owners, however, said they wanted to eat it; and though I offered them a good price, and promised to give them all the meat, there was great hesitation. Suspecting the reason, I offered, though it was night, to set to work immediately and get out the body for them, to which they agreed. The creature was much hacked about, and the two hind feet almost cut off; but it was the largest and finest specimen of the kind I had seen; and after an hour's hard work I handed over the body to the owners, who immediately cut it up and roasted it for supper.

As this was a very good place for birds, I determined to remain a month longer, and took the opportunity of a native boat going to Dobbo, to send Ali for a fresh supply of ammunition and provisions. They started on the 10th of April, and the house was crowded with about a hundred men, boys, women, and girls, bringing their loads of sugar-cane, plantains, sirih-leaf, yams, one lad going from each house to sell the produce and make purchases. The noise was indescribable. At least fifty of the hundred were always talking at once, and that not in the low measured tones of the apathetically polite Malay, but with loud voices, shouts, and screaming laughter, in which the women and children were even more conspicuous than the men. It was only while gazing at me that their tongues were moderately quiet, because their eyes were fully occupied. The black vegetable soil here overlying the coral rock is very rich, and the sugar-cane was finer than any I had ever seen. The canes brought to the boat were often ten and even twelve feet long, and thick in proportion, with short joints throughout, swelling between the knots with the abundance of the rich juice. At Dobbo they get a high price for it, 1d. to 3d. a stick, and there is an insatiable demand among the crews of the praus and the Baba fishermen. Here they eat it continually. They half live on it, and sometimes feed their pigs with it. Near every house are great heaps of the refuse cane; and large wicker-baskets to contain this refuse as it is produced form a regular part of the furniture of a house. Whatever time of the day you enter, you are sure to find three or four people with a yard of cane in one hand, a knife in the other, and a basket between their legs, hacking, paring, chewing, and basket-filling, with a persevering assiduity which reminds one of a hungry cow grazing, or of a caterpillar eating up a leaf.

After five days' absence the boats returned from Dobbo, bringing Ali and all the things I had sent for quite safe. A large party had assembled to be ready to carry home the goods brought, among which were a good many cocoa-nut, which are a great luxury here. It seems strange that they should never plant them; but the reason simply is, that they cannot bring their hearts to bury a good nut for the prospective advantage of a crop twelve years hence. There is also the chance of the fruits being dug up and eaten unless watched night and day. Among the things I had sent for was a box of arrack, and I was now of course besieged with requests for a little drop. I gave them a flask (about two bottles), which was very soon finished, and I was assured that there were many present who had not had a taste. As I feared my box would very soon be emptied if I supplied all their demands, I told them I had given them one, but the second they must pay for, and that afterwards I must have a Paradise bird for each flask. They immediately sent round to all the neighbouring houses, and mustered up a rupee in Dutch copper money, got their second flask, and drunk it as quickly as the first, and were then very talkative, but less noisy and importunate than I had expected. Two or three of them got round me and begged me for the twentieth time to tell them the name of my country. Then, as they could not pronounce it satisfactorily, they insisted that I was deceiving them, and that it was a name of my own invention. One funny old man, who bore a ludicrous resemblance, to a friend of mine at home, was almost indignant. 'Ung-lung!' said he, 'who ever heard of such a name? – ang lang – anger-lung – that can't be the name of your country; you are playing with us.' Then he tried to give a convincing illustration. 'My country is Wanumbai – anybody can say Wanumbai. I'm an orang-Wanumbai; but, N-glung! who ever heard of such a name? Do tell us the real name of your country, and then when you are gone we shall know how to talk about you.' To this luminous argument and remonstrance I could oppose nothing but assertion, and the whole party remained firmly convinced that I was for some reason or other deceiving them. They then attacked me on another point – what all the animals and birds and insects and shells were preserved so carefully for. They had often asked me this before, and I had tried to explain to them that they would be stuffed, and made to look as if alive, and people in my country would go to look at them. But this was not satisfying; in my country there must be many better things to look at, and they could not believe I would take so much trouble with their birds and beasts just for people to look at. They did not want to look at them; and we, who made calico and glass and knives, and all sorts of wonderful things, could not want things from Aru to look at. They had evidently been thinking about it, and had at length got what seemed a very satisfactory theory; for the same old man said to me, in a low, mysterious voice, 'What becomes of them when you go on to the sea?' 'Why, they are all packed up in boxes,' said I 'What did you think became of them?' 'They all come to life again, don't they?' said he; and though I tried to joke it off, and said if they did we should have plenty to eat at sea, he stuck to his opinion, and kept repeating, with an air of deep conviction, 'Yes, they all come to life again, that's what they do – they all come to life again.'

After a little while, and a good deal of talking among themselves, he began again – 'I know all about it – oh yes! Before you came we had rain every day – very wet indeed; now, ever since you have been here, it is fine hot weather. Oh, yes! I know all about it; you can't deceive me.' And so I was set down as a conjurer, and was unable to repel the charge. But the conjurer was completely puzzled by the next question: 'What,' said the old man, 'is the great ship, where the Bugis and

Chinamen go to sell their things? It is always in the great sea – its name is Jong; tell us all about it.' In vain I inquired what they knew about it; they knew nothing but that it was called 'Jong,' and was always in the sea, and was a very great ship, and concluded with, 'Perhaps that is your country?' Finding that I could not or would not tell them anything about 'Jong,' there came more regrets that I would not tell them the real name of my country; and then a long string of compliments, to the effect that I was a much better sort of a person than the Bugis and Chinese, who sometimes came to trade with them, for I gave them things for nothing, and did not try to cheat them. How long would I stop? was the next earnest inquiry. Would I stay two or three months? They would get me plenty of birds and animals, and I might soon finish all the goods I had brought, and then, said the old spokesman, 'Don't go away, but send for more things from Dobbo, and stay here a year or two.' And then again the old story, 'Do tell us the name of your country. We know the Bugis men, and the Macassar men, and the Java men, and the China men; only you, we don't know from what country you come. Ung-lung! it can't be; I know that is not the name of your country.' Seeing no end to this long talk, I said I was tired, and wanted to go to sleep; so after begging – one a little bit of dry fish for his supper, and another a little salt to eat with his sago – they went off very quietly, and I went outside and took a stroll round the house by moonlight, thinking of the simple people and the strange productions of Aru, and then turned in under my mosquito curtain; to sleep with a sense of perfect security in the midst of these good-natured savages.

We now had seven or eight days of hot and dry weather, which reduced the little river to a succession of shallow pools connected by the smallest possible thread of trickling water. If there were a dry season like that of Macassar, the Aru Islands would be uninhabitable, as there is no part of them much above a hundred feet high; and the whole being a mass of porous coralline rock, allows the surface water rapidly to escape. The only dry season they have is for a month or two about September or October, and there is then an excessive scarcity of water, so that sometimes hundreds of birds and other animals die of drought. The natives then remove to houses near the sources of the small streams, where, in the shady depths of the forest, a small quantity of water still remains. Even then many of them have to go miles for their water, which they keep in large bamboos and use very sparingly. They assure me that they catch and kill game of all kinds, by watching at the water holes or setting snares around them. That would be the time for me to make my collections; but the want of water would be a terrible annoyance, and the impossibility of getting away before another whole year had passed made it out of the question.

Ever since leaving Dobbo I had suffered terribly from insects, who seemed here bent upon revenging my long-continued persecution of their race. At our first stopping-place sand-flies were very abundant at night, penetrating to every part of the body, and producing a more lasting irritation than mosquitoes. My feet and ankles especially suffered, and were completely covered with little red swollen specks, which tormented me horribly. On arriving here we were delighted to find the house free from sand-flies or mosquitoes, but in the plantations where my daily walks led me, the day-biting mosquitoes swarmed, and seemed especially to delight in attacking my poor feet. After a month's incessant punishment, those useful members rebelled against such treatment and broke into open insurrection, throwing out numerous inflamed ulcers, which were very painful, and stopped me from walking. So I found myself confined to the house, and with no immediate prospect of leaving it. Wounds or sores in the feet are especially difficult to heal in hot climates, and I therefore dreaded them more than any other illness. The confinement was very annoying, as the fine hot weather was excellent for insects, of which I had every promise of obtaining a fine collection; and it is only by daily and unremitting search that the smaller kinds, and the rarer and more interesting specimens, can be obtained. When I crawled down to the river-side to bathe, I often saw the blue-winged Papilio ulysses, or some other equally rare and beautiful insect; but there was nothing for it but patience, and to return quietly to my bird-skinning, or whatever other work I had indoors. The stings and bites and ceaseless irritation caused by these pests of the tropical forests, would be borne uncomplainingly; but to be kept prisoner by them in so rich and unexplored a country where rare and beautiful creatures are to be met with in every forest ramble – a country reached by such a long and tedious voyage, and which might not in the present century be again visited for the same purpose – is a punishment too severe for a naturalist to pass over in silence.

I had, however, some consolation in the birds my boys brought home daily, more especially the Paradiseas, which they at length obtained in full plumage. It was quite a relief to my mind to get these, for I could hardly have torn myself away from Aru had I not obtained specimens.

But what I valued almost as much as the birds themselves was the knowledge of their habits, which I was daily obtaining both from the accounts of my hunters, and from the conversation of the natives. The birds had now commenced what the people here call their 'sacaleli,' or dancing-parties, in certain trees in the forest, which are not fruit trees as I at first imagined, but which have an immense tread of spreading branches and large but scattered leaves, giving a clear space for the birds to play and exhibit their plumes. On one of these trees a dozen or twenty full-plumaged male birds assemble together, raise up their wings, stretch out their necks, and elevate their exquisite plumes, keeping them in a continual vibration. Between whiles they fly across from branch to branch in great excitement, so that the whole tree is filled with waving plumes in every variety of attitude and motion. The bird itself is nearly as large as a crow, and is of a rich coffee brown colour. The head and neck is of a pure straw yellow above and rich metallic green beneath. The long plumy tufts of golden orange feathers spring from the sides beneath each wing, and when the bird is in repose are partly concealed by them. At the time of its excitement, however, the wings are raised vertically over the back, the head is bent down and stretched out, and the long plumes are raised up and expanded till they form two magnificent golden fans, striped with deep red at the base, and fading off into the pale brown tint of the finely divided and softly waving points. The whole bird is then overshadowed by them, the crouching body, yellow head, and emerald green throat forming but the foundation and setting to the golden glory which waves above. When seen in this attitude, the Bird of Paradise really deserves its name, and must be ranked as one of the most beautiful and most wonderful of living things. I continued also to get specimens of the lovely little king-bird occasionally, as well as numbers of brilliant pigeons, sweet little parroquets, and many curious small birds, most nearly resembling those of Australia and New Guinea.

Here, as among most savage people I have dwelt among, I was delighted with the beauty of the human form – a beauty of which stay-at-home civilized people can scarcely have any conception. What are the finest Grecian statues to the living, moving, breathing men I saw daily around me? The unrestrained grace of the naked savage as he goes about his daily occupations, or lounges at his ease, must be seen to be understood; and a youth bending his bow is the perfection of manly beauty. The women, however, except in extreme youth, are by no means so pleasant to look at as the men. Their strongly-marked features are very unfeminine, and hard work, privations, and very early marriages soon destroy whatever of beauty or grace they may for a short time possess. Their toilet is very simple, but also, I am sorry to say, very coarse, and disgusting. It consists solely of a mat of plaited strips of palm leaves, worn tight round the body, and reaching from the hips to the knees. It seems not to be changed till worn out, is seldom washed, and is generally very dirty. This is the universal dress, except in a few cases where Malay 'sarongs' have come into use. Their frizzly hair is tied in a bunch at the back of the head. They delight in combing, or rather forking it, using for that purpose a large wooden fork with four diverging prongs, which answers the purpose of separating and arranging the long tangled, frizzly mass of cranial vegetation much better than any comb could do. The only ornaments of the women are earrings and necklaces, which they arrange in various tasteful ways. The ends of a necklace are often attached to the earrings, and then looped on to the hair-knot behind. This has really an elegant appearance, the beads hanging gracefully on each side of the head, and by establishing a connection with the earrings give an appearance of utility to those barbarous ornaments. We recommend this style to the consideration of those of the fair sex who still bore holes in their ears and hang rings thereto. Another style of necklace among these Papuan belles is to wear two, each hanging on one side of the neck and under the opposite arm, so as to cross each other. This has a very pretty appearance, in part due to the contrast of the white beads or kangaroo teeth of which they are composed with the dark glossy skin. The earrings themselves are formed of a bar of copper or silver, twisted so that the ends cross. The men, as usual among savages, adorn themselves more than the women. They wear necklaces, earrings, and finger rings, and delight in a band of plaited grass tight round the arm just below the shoulder, to which they attach a bunch of hair or bright coloured feathers by way of ornament. The teeth of small animals, either alone, or alternately with black or white beads, form their necklaces, and sometimes bracelets also. For these latter, however, they prefer brass wire, or the black, horny, wing-spines of the cassowary, which they consider a charm. Anklets of brass or shell, and tight plaited garters below the knee, complete their ordinary decorations.

Some natives of Kobror from further south, and who are reckoned the worst and least civilized of the Aru tribes, came one day to visit us. They have a rather more than usually savage appearance, owing to the greater amount of ornaments they use – the most conspicuous being a large horseshoe-shaped comb which they wear over the forehead, the ends resting on the temples. The back of the comb is fastened into a piece of wood, which is plated with tin in front, and above is attached a plume of feathers from a cock's tail. In other respects they scarcely differed from the people I was living with. They brought me a couple of birds, some shells and insects; showing that the report of the white man and his doing had reached their country. There was probably hardly a man in Aru who had not by this time heard of me.

Besides the domestic utensils already mentioned, the moveable property of a native is very scanty. He has a good supply of spears and bows and arrows for hunting, a parang, or chopping-knife, and an axe – for the stone age has passed away here, owing to the commercial enterprise of the Bugis and other Malay races. Attached to a belt, or hung across his shoulder, he carries a little skin pouch and an ornamented bamboo, containing betel-nut, tobacco, and lime, and a small German wooden-handled knife is generally stuck between his waist-cloth of bark and his bare skin. Each man also possesses a 'cadjan,' or sleeping-mat, made of the broad leaves of a pandanus neatly sewn together in three layers. This mat is about four feet square, and when folded has one end sewn up, so that it forms a kind of sack open at one side. In the closed corner the head or feet can be placed, or by carrying it on the head in a shower it forms both coat and umbrella. It doubles up in a small compass for convenient carriage, and then forms a light and elastic cushion, so that on a journey it becomes clothing, house, bedding, and furniture, all in one.

The only ornaments in an Aru house are trophies of the chase – jaws of wild pigs, the heads and backbones of cassowaries, and plumes made from the feathers of the Bird of Paradise, cassowary, and domestic fowl. The spears, shields, knife-handles, and other utensils are more or less carved in fanciful designs, and the mats and leaf boxes are painted or plaited in neat patterns of red, black, and yellow colours. I must not forget these boxes, which are most ingeniously made of the pith of a balm leaf pegged together, lined inside with pandanus leaves, and outside with the same, or with plaited grass. All the joints and angles are coffered with strips of split rattan sewn neatly on. The lid is covered with the brown leathery spathe of the Areca palm, which is impervious to water, and the whole box is neat, strong, and well finished. They are made from a few inches to two or three feet long, and being much esteemed by the Malay as clothes-boxes, are a regular article of export from Aru. The natives use the smaller ones for tobacco or betel-nut, but seldom have clothes enough to require the larger ones, which are only made for sale.

Among the domestic animals which may generally be seen in native houses, are gaudy parrots, green, red, and blue, a few domestic fowls, which have baskets hung for them to lay in under the eaves, and who sleep on the ridge, and several half-starved wolfish dogs. Instead of rats and mice there are curious little marsupial animals about the same size, which run about at night and nibble anything eatable that may be left uncovered. Four or five different kinds of ants attack everything not isolated by water, and one kind even swims across that; great spiders lurk in baskets and boxes, or hide in the folds of my mosquito curtain; centipedes and millepedes are found everywhere. I have caught them under my pillow and on my head; while in every box, and under every hoard which has lain for some days undisturbed, little scorpions are sure to be found snugly ensconced, with their formidable tails quickly turned up ready for attack or defence. Such companions seem very alarming and dangerous, but all combined are not so bad as the irritation of mosquitoes, or of the insect pests often found at home. These latter are a constant and unceasing source of torment and disgust, whereas you may live a long time among scorpions, spiders, and centipedes, ugly and venomous though they are, and get no harm from them. After living twelve years in the tropics, I have never yet been bitten or stung by either.

The lean and hungry dogs before mentioned were my greatest enemies, and kept me constantly on the watch. If my boys left the bird they were skinning for an instant, it was sure to be carried off. Everything eatable had to be hung up to the roof, to be out of their reach. Ali had just finished skinning a fine King Bird of Paradise one day, when he dropped the skin. Before he could stoop to pick it up, one of this famished race had seized upon it, and he only succeeded in rescuing it from its fangs after it was torn to tatters. Two skins of the large Paradisea, which were quite dry and ready to pack away, were incautiously left on my table for the night, wrapped up in paper. The next morning they were gone, and only a few scattered feathers indicated their fate. My hanging shelf was out of their reach; but having stupidly left a box which served as a step, a full-plumaged Paradise bird was next morning missing; and a dog below the house was to be seen still mumbling over the fragments, with the fine golden plumes all trampled in the mud. Every night, as soon as I was in bed, I could hear them searching about for what they could devour, under my table, and all about my boxes and baskets, keeping me in a state of suspense till morning, lest something of value might incautiously have been left within their reach. They would drink the oil of my floating lamp and eat the wick, and upset or break my crockery if my lazy boys had neglected to wash away even the smell of anything eatable. Bad, however, as they are here, they were worse in a Dyak's house in Borneo where I was once staying, for there they gnawed off the tops of my waterproof boots, ate a large piece out of an old leather game-bag, besides devouring a portion of my mosquito curtain!

April 28th. – Last evening we had a grand consultation, which had evidently been arranged and discussed beforehand. A number of the natives gathered round me, and said they wanted to talk. Two of the best Malay scholars helped each other, the rest putting in hints and ideas in their own language. They told me a long rambling story; but, partly owing to their imperfect knowledge of Malay, partly through my ignorance of local terms, and partly through the incoherence of their narrative, I could not make it out very clearly. It was, however, a tradition, and I was glad to find they had anything of the kind. A long time ago, they said, some strangers came to Aru, and came here to Wanumbai, and the chief of the Wanumbai people did not like them, and wanted them to go away, but they would not go, and so it came to fighting, and many Aru men were killed, and some, along with the chief, were taken prisoners, and carried away by the strangers. Some of the speakers, however, said that he was not carried away, but went away in his own boat to escape from the foreigners, and went to the sea and never came back again. But they all believe that the chief and the people that went with him still live in some foreign country; and if they could but find out where, they would send for them to come back again. Now having some vague idea that white men must know every country beyond the sea, they wanted to know if I had met their people in my country or in the sea. They thought they must be there, for they could not imagine where else they could be. They had sought for them everywhere, they said – on the land and in the sea, in the forest and on the mountains, in the air and in the sky, and could not find them; therefore, they must be in my country, and they begged me to tell them, for I must surely know, as I came from across the great sea. I tried to explain to them that their friends could not have reached my country in small boats; and that there were plenty of islands like Aru all about the sea, which they would be sure to find. Besides, as it was so long ago, the chief and all the people must be dead. But they quite laughed at this idea, and said they were sure they were alive, for they had proof of it. And then they told me that a good many years ago, when the speakers were boys, some Wokan men who were out fishing met these lost people in the sea, and spoke to them; and the chief gave the Wokan men a hundred fathoms of cloth to bring to the men of Wanumbai, to show that they were alive and would soon come back to them, but the Wokan men were thieves, and kept the cloth, and they only heard of it afterwards; and when they spoke about it, the Wokan men denied it, and pretended they had not received the cloth; – so they were quite sure their friends were at that time alive and somewhere in the sea. And again, not many years ago, a report came to them that some Bugis traders had brought some children of their lost people; so they went to Dobbo to see about it, and the owner of the house, who was now speaking to me, was one who went; but the Bugis would not let them see the children, and threatened to kill them if they came into his house. He kept the children shut up in a large box, and when he went away he took them with him. And at the end of each of these stories, they begged me in an imploring tone to tell them if I knew where their chief and their people now were.

By dint of questioning, I got some account of the strangers who had taken away their people. They said they were wonderfully strong, and each one could kill a great many Aru men; and when they were wounded, however badly, they spit upon the place, and it immediately became well. And they made a great net of rattans, and entangled their prisoners in it, and sunk them in the water; and the next day, when they pulled the net up on shore, they made the drowned men come to life again, and carried them away.

Much more of the same kind was told me, but in so confused and rambling a manner that I could make nothing out of it, till I inquired how long ago it was that all this happened, when they told me that after their people were taken away the Bugis came in their praus to trade in Aru, and to buy tripang and birds' nests. It is not impossible that something similar to what they related to me really happened when the early Portuguese discoverers first came to Aru, and has formed the foundation for a continually increasing accumulation of legend and fable. I have no doubt that to the next generation, or even before, I myself shall be transformed into a magician or a demigod, a worker of miracles, and a being of supernatural knowledge. They already believe that all the animals I preserve will come to life again; and to their children it will be related that they actually did so. An unusual spell of fine weather setting in just at my arrival has made them believe I can control the seasons; and the simple circumstance of my always walking alone in the forest is a wonder and a mystery to them, as well as my asking them about birds and animals I have not yet seen, and showing an acquaintance with their form, colours, and habits. These facts are brought against me when I disclaim knowledge of what they wish me to tell them. 'You must know,' say they; 'you know everything: you make the fine weather for your men to shoot, and you know all about our birds and our animals as well as we do; and you go alone into the forest and are not afraid.' Therefore every confession of ignorance on my part is thought to be a blind, a mere excuse to avoid telling them too much. My very writing materials and books are to them weird things; and were I to choose to mystify them by a few simple experiments with lens and magnet, miracles without end would in a few years cluster about me; and future travellers, penetrating to Wanumbai, would hardly believe that a poor English naturalist, who had resided a few months among them, could have been the original of the supernatural being to whom so many marvels were attributed.

For some days I had noticed a good deal of excitement, and many strangers came and went armed with spears and cutlasses, bows and shields. I now found there was war near us – two neighbouring villages having a quarrel about some matter of local politics that I could not understand. They told me it was quite a common thing, and that they are rarely without fighting somewhere near. Individual quarrels are taken up by villages and tribes, and the nonpayment of the stipulated price for a wife is one of the most frequent causes of bitterness and bloodshed. One of the war shields was brought me to look at. It was made of rattans and covered with cotton twist, so as to be both light, strong, and very tough. I should think it would resist any ordinary bullet. About the middle there was an arm-hole with a shutter or flap over it. This enables the arm to be put through and the bow drawn, while the body and face, up to the eyes, remain protected, which cannot be done if the shield is carried on the arm by loops attached at the back in the ordinary way. A few of the young men from our house went to help their friends, but I could not hear that any of them were hurt, or that there was much hard fighting.

May 8th. – I had now been six weeks at Wanumbai, but for more than half the time was laid up in the house with ulcerated feet. My stores being nearly exhausted, and my bird and insect boxes full, and having no immediate prospect of getting the use of my legs again, I determined on returning to Dobbo. Birds had lately become rather scarce, and the Paradise birds had not yet become as plentiful as the natives assured me they would be in another month. The Wanumbai people seemed very sorry at my departure; and well they might be, for the shells and insects they picked up on the way to and from their plantations, and the birds the little boys shot with their bows and arrows, kept them all well supplied with tobacco and gambir, besides enabling them to accumulate a stock of beads and coppers for future expenses. The owner of the house was supplied gratis with a little rice, fish, or salt, whenever he asked for it, which I must say was not very often. On parting, I distributed among them my remnant stock of salt and tobacco, and gave my host a flask of arrack, and believe that on the whole my stay with these simple and good-natured people was pro- ductive of pleasure and profit to both parties. I fully intended to come back; and had I known that circum- stances would have prevented my doing so, shoed have felt some sorrow in leaving a place where I had first seen so many rare and beautiful living things, and had so fully enjoyed the pleasure which fills the heart of the naturalist when he is so fortunate as to discover a district hitherto unexplored, and where every day brings forth new and unexpected treasures. We loaded our boat in the afternoon, and, starting before day- break, by the help of a fair wind reached Dobbo late the same evening.

THE STORY OF PENGUIN CLASSICS

Before 1946 …'Classics' are mainly the domain of academics and students, without readable editions for everyone else. This all changes when a little-known classicist, E. V. Rieu, presents Penguin founder Allen Lane with the translation of Homer's *Odyssey* that he has been working on and reading to his wife Nelly in his spare time.

1946 *The Odyssey* becomes the first Penguin Classic published, and promptly sells three million copies. Suddenly, classic books are no longer for the privileged few.

1950s Rieu, now series editor, turns to professional writers for the best modern, readable translations, including Dorothy L. Sayers's *Inferno* and Robert Graves's *The Twelve Caesars*, which revives the salacious original.

1960s The Classics are given the distinctive black jackets that have remained a constant throughout the series's various looks. Rieu retires in 1964, hailing the Penguin Classics list as 'the greatest educative force of the 20th century'.

1970s A new generation of translators arrives to swell the Penguin Classics ranks, and the list grows to encompass more philosophy, religion, science, history and politics.

1980s The Penguin American Library joins the Classics stable, with titles such as *The Last of the Mohicans* safeguarded. Penguin Classics now offers the most comprehensive library of world literature available.

1990s The launch of Penguin Audiobooks brings the classics to a listening audience for the first time, and in 1999 the launch of the Penguin Classics website takes them online to a larger global readership than ever before.

The 21st Century Penguin Classics are rejacketed for the first time in nearly twenty years. This world famous series now consists of more than 1300 titles, making the widest range of the best books ever written available to millions – and constantly redefining the meaning of what makes a 'classic'.

The Odyssey continues …

The best books ever written

PENGUIN ⏺ CLASSICS

SINCE 1946

Find out more at www.penguinclassics.com